Small Group
Know How

BRYN HUGHES

MONARCH
BOOKS

MILL HILL, LONDON NW7 3SA & GRAND RAPIDS, MICHIGAN 49501

First published by Monarch Books in the UK in 2001,
Concorde House, Grenville Place, Mill Hill, London NW7 3SA.

Distributed by:
UK: STL, PO Box 300, Kingstown Broadway,
Carlisle, Cumbria CA3 0QS;
USA: Kregel Publications, PO Box 2607,
Grand Rapids, Michigan 49501.

ISBN 1 85424 524 4 (UK)
ISBN 0 8254 6030 1 (USA)

British Library Cataloguing Data
A catalogue record for this book is available
from the British Library.

Designed and produced for the publisher by
Gazelle Creative Productions,
Concorde House, Grenville Place, Mill Hill,
London NW7 3SA.

To Pete Carter,
Leader of the North Kent Community Church,
my home church.

Words cannot express my thanks for his friendship, care and wisdom. His encouragement and ministry have had a massive impact on the lives of Vicky and me. He walks the talk with great integrity, truly leading by example in every way. The fact that he supports Chelsea should be forgiven by all true football supporters, since it is his most blatant weakness!

Acknowledgements

Many thanks to Chris Cartwright, David Cormack, Tim Goss, Helen Hawkins, Tony Horsfall, Alan Preston and Nigel Ring — for their hard work in proof-reading and for such constructive comments. Their work has brought vital contributions to this book in different ways, as experts in cell church, church leadership, or in their own writing skills. My thanks in every case also, for their friendship and understanding.

I'm grateful to Alan Meyer, Pastor of Carlisle Elim Church, for his experience and sharp insights as their church changed its structures. Many thanks, too, to Gill Brentford for the Foreword.

Contents

Foreword   6

Introduction   7

PART 1   **UNDERSTANDING SMALL GROUPS**

Chapter 1   Small Groups in the Church Today   11

Chapter 2   Developing Small Groups   21

Chapter 3   Caring Through Small Groups   34

PART 2   **LEADING SMALL GROUPS**

Chapter 4   The Qualities of a Good Small-group Leader   45

Chapter 5   Preparing More Group Leaders   58

Chapter 6   The Responsibilities of Being a Small-group Leader   70

Chapter 7   Clarifying the Small-group Purpose   79

Chapter 8   Consistent Values   88

Chapter 9   Vision   100

PART 3   **THE SKILLS OF SMALL-GROUP LEADERSHIP**

Chapter 10   Transitioning of Structures   111

Chapter 11   Leading Discussions and Asking Questions   123

Chapter 12   Listening   131

Chapter 13   Handling Tricky Situations   139

Chapter 14   Evaluating the Small Group   148

Conclusion   157

Bibliography   160

Foreword

I met Bryn when I attended my first 'Christians in Management' course at Pitlochry in Scotland. He was one of the trainers. During that time I was stimulated, challenged and learnt a lot. It gave me an insight into Bryn's special gift of relating his teaching and training skills to an individual or a group's need of the moment.

At a time in the Church when small groups of all kinds are seen to be crucial to its future and where the distinctions between such groups and 'cell church' are sometimes blurred, this book is timely. Bryn's analysis of the critical differences between cells and bible groups, fellowship and prayer groups makes clear what particular component of "being Church" is the distinctive feature of each group.

Christ spent much of his ministry with a small group of twelve. They became the pioneers of the early Church and models of its leadership. But it is from St.Paul's teaching in Ephesians that Bryn draws the central model for his analysis. We are all aware just how much we need the power of God when leading our small groups, but the consciousness of that need should drive us more diligently to learn the skills we so badly need to lead them more effectively. I believe that is just what Bryn has done by giving us the toolbox of skills he lays out here.

Many of these insights will not be new. However, each of them has been focussed and honed for this particular task. Bryn has drawn on all his experience, his understanding of relationships and his knowledge to give us a set of tools which each of us, however experienced, cannot fail to find helpful.

Gill Brentford,
Sussex, January 2001.

Introduction

This book is designed as a practical guide for improving the small groups in your church. The content is appropriate for any church with small groups, whether you have a home-group focus or are a cell church. I've taken account of cell churches, and most chapters make specific reference to them, but this is not a book about cell church. There will be practical ideas for group leaders and trainee group leaders, my main target readership, as well as for the senior ministers or elders within any congregation. Good small groups require a concerted approach to development from the whole church leadership; although some chapters may seem to be principally directed at one of eldership, group leaders or trainee group leaders, I really want all these levels of leadership to share the concepts and responsibility for improvement.

In recent years, a new structure called cell church has emerged which has served many congregations well. At the time of writing, the best available statistics indicate about 700 churches linked to "Cell Church UK". About 400 churches would deem themselves "cell churches" already, or be actively moving to adopt that structure. Among the 700 churches, there are approximately:

Anglican churches:	150 to 200
Baptist churches:	50-60
Methodist, URC and Catholic:	Less than 10 in total
"New" churches and Pentecostal:	Over 300

(My thanks to Laurence Singlehurst for this information.)

The numbers involved still represent a very small percentage of all the churches across the UK. A far greater number of churches include homegroups within their strategy and programme, and these may appear under a variety of titles. The similarities and differences between homegroups and cells are both clear and interesting.

An understanding of cell church depends on which "guru" you read, and to a lesser extent, when you take your snapshot. Initially, the principal difference between cell and other churches was that the small-group meeting was one of the two central elements of church life, not an optional bolt-on extra. The larger gathering still had a place in the programme, usually referred to as a "celebration"; it was a valuable meeting where the cells met together. Not only is the cell-church phenomenon a relatively new structure within the UK, but it is also a completely fresh paradigm that requires a change of mentality and culture to make it successful. By many criteria, most cell churches are doing very well.

Very little new terminology is necessary to understand this book if you are not in a cell church, but there are a few concepts with which some readers may not be familiar. For example, in a cell church there are:

Zone pastors:	A tier of leadership, each pastor overseeing a few cells.
Interns:	Assistant cell leaders, in the post with the expectation that they will soon lead a cell themselves.
The four "W"s:	The content of a cell evening usually contains four ingredients — Welcome, Worship, Word and Works/Witness.

The cell structure expects numerical growth and when a cell is too big, an additional group is formed. This process is called *multiplying*, not dividing!

Throughout the text I have referred to the "celebration" as the Sunday meeting, and whether they are cells or homegroups, I have assumed that these small groups meet on a mid-week evening. However, I recognise that some cells meet on a Sunday morning (yes, the paradigm shift is as dramatic as that); and some homegroups meet on Sunday evenings or mid-week during the daytime. I hope that there is no additional jargon needed to make complete sense of the text, whatever your church background and experience.

The cell-church phenomenon has caused many of us to rethink our attitude and approach to small groups. But there is no reason why it needed to become a "movement". Most of the recent literature about small groups within the UK has been devoted to cells, and believe me, there are lorry-loads of materials! There is a great deal of passion from the advocates. This book is partly designed to bring some balance to the debate, recognizing what cell with its differences has done for many churches, but also looking at how homegroups can be improved without going the whole hog. For instance, citing ground that we will consider more carefully later, homegroups could always have been made more outward looking and we should have always been training the next raft of small-group leaders. Probably cell has been adopted in this country because we weren't doing some of the things that we could and should have been doing within the old structures.

Devotees of cell generally reckon that you need to adopt the whole package for any prospect of "success" and would not stress the similarities with homegroups. Yet if adoption is all or nothing, why are some churches that have implemented cell coming out so differently from others? As time goes by, these differences between cell churches are becoming more pronounced and more divergent. The variations are noticeable even within streams of what used to be called "the house church" movement, as well as from one denomination to another.

As I said at the outset, while this book may contribute to balance, debate and understanding, my prime aim is that any church with small groups will find tools for improving those groups. Hence I have used very few references and quotations; my aim is not to play previous contributors off against each other, neither is argument my mode of influence. The theoretical research has been done; by choice, the detail is omitted, for the sake of simplicity. My views are based on fifteen years in a training and consultancy role to churches and I have been very privileged in the range of churches where I have worked.

Chapter *1*

Small Groups in the Church Today

I want to consider the similarities and the differences between the cell-church concept and what we have more traditionally called homegroups. Please be careful how you interpret the words as other people use them. The terms themselves are not so critical as what we mean by the terms and that deserves exploration. I've found that people probably use the term homegroups with greater agreed meaning than when the conversation turns to cells; Bible study is usually the central component, often with some measure of worship and prayer. There are just as many variations in how cell is interpreted. I can take you to cell churches where the evening programme is centrally determined and then distributed to the cell leaders for implementation, even prescribing which choruses should be sung. In other churches that I have visited, cell leaders are given very considerable autonomy. Some churches have extended the cell structure to the youth and children's departments whereas others have not. Some churches augment the cells with additional programmes while some attempt most of the church functions via the cells. There are many variations on the general themes.

There ought to be nothing new in the *foundations* of church life. God's revelation to His people via the Bible is complete and timeless. The challenge to the church today is not to make his word relevant; it always has been and always will be relevant, but we need to show its application.

In different cultures and in different times, there should be different appropriate expressions of church life to show this relevance. With any new initiative, we need to look again at Scripture, in the first instance, for our guidelines.

There will be the *rhema* word in all seasons as well as the *logos* word. God will continue to speak prophetically and reveal himself to his people. For possible examples, and dependent on personal theology, we might cite seasons of revelation on deliverance, inner healing and the so-called Toronto blessing. The new churches have moved from being insular to outward looking and now have a fresh emphasis on "mercy ministries" to the poor and needy. For the real benefits, all of these possible examples of revelation have to be integrated into the bigger picture, our understanding based on his timeless word. Yet despite our reliance on Scripture and these apparently significant landmarks, there is still colossal scope for valid variations within the evangelical wing of the church. For example, the New Testament is imprecise about the structures, methodology and form of church. All denominations would claim to be biblical and yet have devised widely varying interpretations of church governance, let alone the spectrum within those denominations, or our chosen stances on smaller issues.

Take another concept like teamwork. The word can legitimately mean very different things to different people. You can make out a case for teamworking from Scripture or equally build an argument for the sole, autocratic leader. Neither position would be totally convincing to the opposite faction. In one church where I was working as a consultant, I failed to communicate on this key topic of teamworking with the minister for about 18 months; we were using the word "team" to mean totally different things. I meant joint decision-making; he meant a squad of the busiest people in the church. That cross-communication was a lesson that I have never forgotten. To quote a similar example of the use of Scripture, I have heard far more exposition of tithing (from Malachi 3) than I have about the year of jubilee (from Leviticus 25), yet the scale of biblical evidence seems similar.

Dare I say that I suspect that much of the use of Scripture in debates about church life is to illustrate a chosen position rather than as the initial source and foundation of that position? Most of us are pretty selective about the weight we give to certain verses and passages as well as being capable of dismissing great inconvenient chunks of Scripture as only appropriate to the times in which they were written.

We need to apply the same level of analysis to small groups; any conclusions need to be based on a substantial weight of biblical evidence, not just on a few loosely linked verses. In recent years the practice of cell-church structures has become more frequent in the United Kingdom. Many books on the subject of cells and small groups start with a New Testament selection of verses. Without the concepts being manifestly and overtly biblical, groups cannot be claimed to be the panacea to all the problems of church life. But pragmatically I am absolutely convinced that effective, growing churches need to have a strong emphasis on small groups. Most really healthy churches in the UK have a thriving small-group programme. I conclude that:

> **THE BIBLICAL EVIDENCE FOR SMALL GROUPS IS NOT OVERWHELMING.**
> **THE PRAGMATIC REASONS ARE COMPREHENSIVE AND COMPELLING.**

The principles of cell church

So what are the core non-negotiable principles of the cell church? Where is the distinctiveness? First, there must be an emphasis on numerical growth. The indicative language is definitely about the cells multiplying, rather than dividing! Secondly, a decisive issue is whether the small group is a valid, integral or central part of church life. In cell churches the small group must be pivotal. Recent literature has increasingly focused on the importance of discipleship.

Essentially, cell church must not only be a structure, but a culture or a mentality. Industry and other organisations are littered with disasters where the structures have been changed without the accompanying mindset, which is necessary for successful implementation. Patterns of thinking change more slowly than structures and we will look at how to approach a process of transition in Chapter 10.

We also need to remember that although the cell concept has been around for some time (I have found references in 1979), we have little formal research on a substantial scale within our culture. There is no guarantee that what works in Asia can be adopted wholesale into our Western world. Certainly there are signs that there is pleasing numerical growth in many churches that have gone the cell route, but there cannot be a parallel control group to validate the statistics. How do we know that the same results would not have been achieved with a different structure but the same leadership? (Statistics, especially when the data is limited, can be used to prove anything. We might be facing similar dangers to the old story that ice cream causes drowning. The evidence is very convincing because the correlation on a daily basis between ice-cream sales and drowning is high; the link being good weather!)

I understand the uniqueness of cell-church structures and thinking. I visit, ask questions, study and experience many cell churches within my ministry. But I feel the need to underline the similarities as well as the differences. There was no reason why homegroups could not have been designed for evangelism. We should always have been training the next cluster of small-group leaders; now in cell churches we call them interns. There are some materials to help with discipleship, especially of new converts; cell church now talks of equipping tracks. Sadly we have needed the challenge of new structures to force us into revisiting our core values, and even asking us to remember what church is all about, down to its ultimate purposes.

THE TRUTH IS THAT WE WERE NOT DOING MANY OF THE THINGS THAT WE SAID WE HELD DEAR, TO ANYTHING LIKE THE RIGHT LEVEL.

The biggest benefit that I have seen in cell churches is a change in the expectations of the average member. Many apparent passengers have become competent foot soldiers. Levels of effectiveness have leapt forward dramatically across a wide spectrum of many church memberships. My principal remaining concern about cells is that a certain level of leadership is not being developed because the "career path" of intern, cell-group leader to zone pastor does not identify or touch a raft of people with particular gift portfolios and leadership potential.

Functions and numbers

What can be done exclusively in either big groups or small ones? What can be undertaken whatever the size of the gathering? You can worship in a big group, or in a small number and obviously alone. For many people, worshipping in a small group is a trifle disconcerting; the noise level, or lack of it, feels strange. There is the tendency for people to feel exposed for "how" rather than "why" and "what" they are singing. But there is no biblical reason for narrowing worship to the Sunday meeting; it's just that historically we were more comfortable with the larger group style and expression. Increasingly we are recognizing that we don't have to be bound by that historical expectation.

We can teach, and learn, in different-sized groups. The

style needs to be adapted so that it is appropriate for the group size. The traditional sermon is a teaching tool to vast numbers and there are other methods of learning apart from this "lecture" style more suitable for a small group. (Perhaps now is not the time to explore this issue but I have suspicions about which context produces the greater fruit!) We can worship, teach and learn in any group size. To establish the importance of small groups we need to consider the benefits which can be achieved in no other setting. For example:

> To build some closer relationships within the church.
> To grow in Christ by expressing gifts.
> To evangelize in a way that is uniquely acceptable to some unsaved people.

Especially:

**YOU CANNOT BUILD RELATIONSHIPS IN A BIG GROUP.
EVEN WITH COFFEE AFTER THE SERVICE, SUNDAY MORNING
IS NOT A FORUM FOR BUILDING RELATIONSHIPS.**

Levels of intimacy

One of the challenges to developing community within our churches is to master the paradox of intimacy. People come into a small-group context with two conflicting emotions at play inside them. They recognize both the desire and need for close relationships, but at the same time they are hesitant about being vulnerable and transparent. The experience of some people is that others let them down, especially when they bare their souls; any desire to trust has taken many buffetings.

Jesus is clearly recorded as having different degrees of intimacy. Peter, James and John were the closest cluster, then the remainder of the twelve, followed by the seventy. In our culture and lifestyle there are also realistic limits;

relationships require time for initiation and cultivation. Most of us probably sustain only a few intimate friendships, then there is a larger group with whom we can share and offer mutual support. This limit is as good a reason for establishing the maximum size of a small group as any other reason. Not only do group dynamics indicate a plateau of about twelve people, but also we are unlikely to be able to sustain much level of relationship beyond that figure. The third level of contact has a broad possible numerical range and covers function more than real friendship; we know the people well enough to work together. The fourth and final group range is as wide as you like and offers no more than a greeting with a fervent hope that we can remember their name!

In reverse order, the levels of intimacy would be characterized by the type of communication between the parties. In the most cursory style, conversation revolves around factual information, like the weather, football and prices at the shop. With a closer group of friends, the conversation progressively contains personal information and the interpretation of events. The ultimate level with the few people who are close to us is the forum where feelings can also be revealed.

In our lounge, there is a feature brick wall and a fireplace. (Or else the plasterer had run out of materials!) The wall reminds me of the church; I can draw a parallel between the people of the church and my wall. Each brick touches six other bricks, there are more bricks within the same wall, and many bricks that are recognized to be part of the same building but which are based some distance away. The small group is the only *formalized* opportunity within the church which encourages the building of friendships.

Principles of small-group dynamics

We ought to view leading a small group as a spiritual activity obviously, but also as both an art and a science. No two groups are alike, and yet there are general rules that seem to apply to the majority of small groups. That is not to say that all of these principles will apply to your group all of the time. This list is an adaptation of a longer one quoted by many authors.

1. The initial reasons for joining a small group are at least partially self-centred. People will sustain their attendance if their needs continue to be met.
2. People prefer groups with other members who are similar in age, attitudes, abilities and needs. Members feel much easier in a relatively homogeneous group than facing the challenge of managing differences.
3. There will be less time for each individual to participate in a larger group. This may suit some people who are naturally reserved, but disappoint others.
4. Group size has an effect on the style of leadership. In cells, the expectation is that leadership roles are often shared. In other types of group, there may be a greater tendency for one dominant leader as the group size increases.
5. The physical setting of the group meeting has a significant impact on group dynamics and behaviour and therefore on process and effectiveness.
6. The length of time since salvation does not have a direct correlation with the effectiveness of a member. Sometimes the fresh expectations of new Christians are particularly constructive. Long-standing members may oppose a change to new structures like cells because of their personal histories.
7. A clear understanding of the purpose of the group and its processes will greatly increase effectiveness.
8. Relationships are enhanced when the group share the goal setting and also take part in reviewing their progress.

9. Members who are perceived to be senior in status (eg a "full-time" Christian worker) have more freedom to deviate from the group norms without sanctions. New members are expected to "toe the line".
10. Shared leadership, in whatever form, promotes greater conformity to norms and the corporate culture.

Structures

The choice of structure will not be the single feature most likely to influence the effectiveness of the church. The quality of the leadership is the highest-ranking factor. But, for a given leadership team, the structures chosen may have a major effect. In contrasting homegroups and cells we are looking at two of the possible structures for church life. There is no such thing as an inherently good structure or a bad one; its value depends on what you are trying to achieve. Structure therefore is subordinate to vision. If you know where you hope to be going, then there is a rationale for adopting some structures more than others.

There will remain the tricky issue of how we allocate people to groups, whatever structure is adopted. The task is without end as people leave the church, or newcomers join it, and personalities dictate that somebody will always be wanting to change from one group to another. The usual methods of assigning people to groups are by geography, maturity, choice or the desire that all groups should reflect the full spectrum of the church society. There is no absolute reason for one method in a cell church and another rationale in homegroups. All methods of allocation are possible for any structure with a small-group programme. Often the presumption about cells is that the groups draw on all the range of people in the church, but in practice there are often variations. For example, people who have come through an Alpha group together may become a cell as soon as the Alpha course is finished.

In summary:

1. The pragmatic case for small groups is overwhelming. There is no additional biblical basis for any one particular structure.

2. There are some elements of church life best undertaken in small groups.

3. There are some general principles governing small-group dynamics that are well researched and tested.

4. Cell mentality depends on values not just structures, and the adoption of cells must be approached accordingly.

5. In recent years we have highlighted the philosophical differences of cell churches. There are also many similarities between cells and homegroups. I have listed some of them here with the chapter headings for later reference:

- Good pastoral care is potentially best organized via small groups. (Chapter 3)
- We need to give much more attention to developing future group leaders. (Chapter 5)
- Any group needs to know their purpose and core values. (Chapters 7–8)
- All groups need a medium-term vision. (Chapter 9)
- There are some core skills of small-group dynamics and leadership. (Chapters 11–14)

Chapter **2**

Developing Small Groups

The experience of cell churches, including many outside the UK, offers some easily transferable concepts. The four "W"s are now quoted repeatedly in the cell-church philosophy. They give a blueprint for the contents of a cell-group meeting and are:

Welcome
Worship
Word
Works/Witness.

Not surprisingly, they are something of a summary of the eternal purposes of the church, which we will explore in Chapter 7. If the cell is designed to encapsulate much of church life, then all of the purposes will be represented during an evening. However, while the four "W"s are not sacred, God's foundations and the purposes of his church are non-negotiable. The four "W"s are a useful format and guideline but it is good to keep other alternatives and options in mind, particularly when we have biblical instruction on them. For example: "From him the whole body, joined and held together by every supporting ligament, grows and builds itself up in love, as each part does its work" (Ephesians 4:16). This verse provides a practical way of developing small groups and a checklist to see whether the small group is functioning adequately or not.

Years ago, when I was a choirboy in an Anglican church, I frequently read one of the lessons. My general approach was that if I was to read from the Old Testament, I prepared carefully: there might be long words and difficult names of people or places. When the reading was from the New Testament, I could afford to skimp on the homework. This lazy rule of thumb failed me abruptly one day; the passage was Ephesians 4 and I can't remember which translation was on the lectern. However, I do recall being decidedly short of breath as I anticipated the end of a sentence, only to find that there were very few breaks in the first sixteen verses! The memory has stayed with me and always reminds me that the last few verses of this section are inextricably linked to the earlier verses; the whole reason for this wonderful parallel between the church and a physical body is ultimately encapsulated in verse 16. I have used verses 14 to 16 countless times in training teams and small-group leaders. The seven verbs of verse 16, with a tiny bit of poetic grammatical licence, are the summary of the body functioning smoothly and they are easily memorized:

JOINING
HOLDING
SUPPORTING
GROWING
BUILDING
LOVING
WORKING.

The principles can be applied equally to whole churches and small groups.

1. Joining

In some ways, sports clubs, organizations and churches have a similarity in that there will often be a distinction between members and non-members. Different denominations have different procedures for acceptance into membership. In Baptist churches, there would usually be an interview with a couple of the deacons, a vote at the full church meeting, and then a formal welcome and handshake at a Sunday service. The key event for Anglicans is less obvious; the confirmation service symbolizes entry into the worldwide communion, rather than into membership of a particular parish church. With membership in the military you acquire a uniform, in other organizations a badge or an identity card.

In the "newer" churches, I have found that roughly half the churches have a formal membership system; others take the stance that "full involvement" is a more meaningful way of recognizing "joined-ness". Often the key criterion of membership used to be that a person attends the small-group meeting on a mid-week evening. That yardstick is inappropriate in a cell church because visiting the small group is often the first experience of the church, not the last and optional extra. Their experience is "belonging before believing". The combined attendance in small groups may well exceed the number meeting in the larger celebration forum. The experience of joining is changing.

Many churches of all styles now have some sort of commitment course, ranging from a few weeks to a few months. There is great merit in this approach because the course offers the new person an opportunity to understand what membership means in this particular local expression of church. When we have not taught good membership to newcomers sufficiently well, conflicts arise later because the new members' pre-conceptions of church were not what the community had designed and were providing. There are far more books about leadership than membership, yet there should be more Indians than chiefs! It is vital that new members understand the values and vision at the end of the commitment process. Ceremonies are important but there is much more to joining than just the special moment. A graft on a tree takes a few minutes but the process of becoming one tree takes at least a season. Research into organizations indicates that fully joining a new organization takes between one and two years and that the effectiveness of the join, graft and integration depends on the quality of the joining process. Church is no exception. Membership must have tangible expression if it is to be meaningful.

We need to remember that first impressions are powerful and lasting. For example, in job interviews the decision about most candidates who are rejected is made within the first five minutes. If you go on a Christian camp or weekend conference, delegates say that the ambience is established within the first few minutes; that's when the whole trip is made or broken for them. In a similar way, newcomers to a small group are very impressionable in the first few minutes of their very first meeting. So the type of action that might be illustrative of effective and sympathetic "joining" includes:

> A comfortable chair, especially if it is a full room.
> Introductions to other people.
> Asking them to introduce themselves.
> Involving them very personally, but not putting them on the spot too early.
> Answering any questions about the wider church honestly, but without too much detail.

2. Holding

This is the one verb for which I prefer other translations to the NIV; the phrase "knit together" is very graphic and describes the integration that we should be aiming towards. As any evangelist will tell you, finding new people and keeping them are two different issues. I'm not talking about the natural turnover as people move because of job requirements, family commitments, health or retirement.

We need to consider the folk who, having made a degree of commitment, maybe not only to God but also to your particular small group, later decide to move out or on. Their initial experience is that of being babes in Christ. It's a wonderful time; they are the focus of attention, they get top-quality milk and their nappies are changed for them! (In spiritual terms, obviously!) But then (hopefully!), there is another fresh person joining and they are no longer the new babe on the block, the focus of all that lavish care. Now they are just A. N. Other, but the least known, possessing the least track record and therefore the least trusted of the regular membership. This is a very vulnerable time, not for the group but for A. N. Other.

Typical activities that we need to do during this "holding" phase include:

Watching out for the first signs of wavering.
Noticing less frequent attendance.
Checking the Christian status of the rest of the family.
Asking about any potential transport difficulty to meetings.
Observing on Sunday whether others are chatting to them in the wider context.
Making sure that they are still receiving invitations of hospitality.

3. Supporting

Support is a two-way issue. Group leaders will regularly be asked to give support to others but I want to emphasize that it is necessary for the leader to look for support as well. Leadership can often be a lonely business. Jesus had an inner team of three within the twelve disciples; more was offered to them but also a little more was asked of them. We read of no bad feeling from the outer nine to the inner three. Only Mrs Zebedee had any status problems with the way that Jesus conducted the team affairs! As a strong general principle, I believe that leaders should be prepared to look for internal support from within their group. If, as a leader, you cannot model vulnerability and disclosure to other people, then you have no right to expect these features from the members.

Let's now look at the way in which we offer support. I want to link challenge and support in a diagram that has critical implications for the life of the group. Challenge and support should be balanced.

High support

smothered
molly-coddled
frustrated
bored
low risk

learning
excitement
growth
fulfilment

Low challenge

High challenge

apathetic
lethargic
zero growth

isolated
fearful
lonely
exposed
vulnerable

Low support

There are four possible scenarios to the matrix of **Support** and **Challenge**. Our goal is for people to be experiencing high challenge together with appropriate support, as in the top right-hand corner of the diagram. The worst option is the bottom left quadrant; as the old joke says, "There's a lot of apathy around, but then, nobody seems to care!" The other two corners can be frequently found and are produced by very different styles of leadership. It's a key question for you to answer now: which box on the graph are you most likely to generate? Do you tend to offer more support than challenge or the other way round? Would your group members give the same answer? The climate that these quadrants create and represent will be a key factor in determining how much members enjoy your group and how much they will grow within it.

Activities linked with "supporting" might include:

Listening.
Engaging in low-level maintenance-style pastoral care.
Asking questions that show concern.
Offering and asking for help to meet practical needs.
Showing an interest in the whole person.
Sharing successes and failures.

Activities associated with challenge are similar to those under the next section, the fourth verb.

4. Growing

It is clear from Scripture that God wants us to grow; hence the gift of the Holy Spirit. But it is also clear that not everybody recognizes the need for growth and for some personality types, growth will matter more than for others. Suppose that I was to move to your area with a company job posting, and we knew that I would be based there throughout a five-year contract. I would want the secure knowledge that in your church and group I would have the opportunity to develop, and that I would acquire new skills and more proficiency in existing skills, and that my gifts would have the freedom to flourish among you. I would accept that there will be an early stage when I am getting my feet under the table and you are getting to know me. That will be fine as long as I can see evidence that others are growing and that in time you will have the same expectations of me.

Unfortunately, that scenario would not be true for everyone; all church members do not seem to want to grow in this way. Sadly, I think the common reason for this state of affairs is that often people have no experience or expectation of growing within church life, and so therefore they don't. It's a self-fulfilling prophecy. Churches and leaders have concentrated for too long on the commitment that they expect from members, as though "growing" individuals is incompatible with the needs of the body as a whole. Happily, the balance between individual needs and the corporate purpose is not quite the dichotomy that many leaders anticipate. Fulfilled members make for effective groups and churches.

Providing a climate for "growing" should include:

Offering opportunities in any form of ministry beyond proven experience and ability.

Discussing with people how they hope to develop the expression of their gifts.

Engaging in serious Bible study, and sharing what God is saying at a personal level.

Encouraging fewer extreme "high" and "low" phases in their Christian walk.

Recognizing and providing the many ways in which people can grow.

Encouraging initiative taking.

Handling mistakes in a positive way.

5. Building

The author of Ephesians has chosen to distinguish between growing and building. As we have seen above, growing is an individual activity and does not need chemistry with other members (although these dynamics may well help growth). If I were stranded on a desert island, I would probably grow. My prayer life might get more attention and I might become a real expert on the berries that are good for you and those that cause short-term damage! But I would not be able to build. This dimension needs other people to interact with and who will grind at my rough edges; I can't do it solo.

Another facet of building within the small group is linked to synergy. The group can be better than the sum of its parts; two plus two can make five! Iron sharpening iron, the creative and the evaluative needing each other, the evangelist and the pastor recognizing that the body would be very incomplete without the different contributions. The nub of group dynamics is that "different means I need you, although I may not always find you comfortable!"

But Ephesians 4:16 does not just say "building". It talks about the body "building itself up". This is a spiritual phenomenon and unfortunately many teams, groups and organizations do quite the opposite; they knock themselves down. Groups take a certain amount of energy just to stand still, dealing with things like administration and minor pastoral needs. The ability of a group to build itself up is the spiritual synergy that means that nobody need be exhausted by striving to make the dynamics happen; everybody can arrive a little tired and go away the stronger through the interaction.

Building together needs the fun component as well. I know that "the group that prays together, stays together" but it is also true that the group that plays together stays together. Social activities should be an integral part of the team dynamics and eating food together is a fairly intimate activity. As the Alpha course has shown us, meals can combine serious spiritual business with a very enjoyable time. Remember that we might not even want the group to stay together for too long, if we are expecting the group to multiply within two years.

In summary, "building" should include:

Group social activities.
The use of spiritual gifts that require mutual dependence.
Learning to appreciate complementary ways of thinking.
Fun and laughter!

6. Loving

Much could be, and has been said on this subject, and therefore I want to emphasize only one aspect. Loving must be on the other person's terms. Too often I suspect, our acts of kindness are not really based on a knowledge of their preferences, but on what we think that love should look like to them. Actions are then about our definition of love and are not personalized as an act to bless that particular member in a unique way.

Let me give you an example. Suppose two people in our group had been particularly encouraging to us, by faithfully praying for our ministry. As a "thank you" my wife and I buy them each a box of chocolates. Probably they would receive that as a loving gesture. But in time as we begin to know them better, we might find out that one member really does like chocolates, although they much prefer plain, while the other finds a bunch of flowers a much greater blessing. Now our love can move from a general demonstration based on our presumptions, to something more personal and specific.

Under "loving" we also need to consider deep friendships. What depth of relationship do you really share with your group? How many people matter to you far more than the task, the joint enterprise in hand? Would you consider going on holiday together with another family in your group? What is the evidence to an outsider that the quality of relationships in the church is better than what the world is offering?

"Loving" might include:

Acts of kindness.
Affirming of the person, not just approval of a well-done task.
Remembering birthdays.
Sticking with them when their weaknesses become more apparent.

Any expression of "one anothering".

Assuming that they are the next generation of leaders, and acting accordingly.

Valuing your people and respecting their differences.

7. Working

These last two verbs, loving and working, are reversed in some translations, but I prefer this order. Groups do need clarity in their task if they are going to experience a sense of satisfaction and I would be the first to want us to clarify the purpose of meeting together. You don't get a happy football team who are not even sure of the score! But frequently I am finding the greater danger in groups today is that they only look at the output of the group and ignore the dynamics illustrated by the other six verbs.

If we wish to ensure that the "working" is happening, we should pay attention to these types of issues:

Encouraging faithfulness, completing what the group says it will do.

Having a sense of purpose in the wider church involvement, outside the small group.

Being net contributors to the life of the church, not expecting church to always succour them.

Ensuring individual contributions are thoroughly harnessed and subordinated to the present vision of the church.

Providing role definition and clarity.

Beginning to utilize strengths and produce mastercrafters rather than producing "Jacks of all trades".

It is very easy to envisage the problems that a group will face if we are weak in providing any of these components:

If we are weak in:	The predictable outcome will be:
JOINING	No numerical growth. Visitors, not members. Low sense of identity.
HOLDING	We lose as many as we gain. Low external image and reputation. Murmuring and discontent.
SUPPORTING	Leader is exposed and vulnerable. Members feel support not sufficient for tasks. Low trust levels.
GROWING	Spiritual stagnation. No personal vision. Bored with the mundane.
BUILDING	Individualism and independence. Low cohesion. No sense of community.
LOVING	Results at the cost of people. No different experience from the world. People feeling used.
WORKING	Low emphasis on achievements. High turnover because of low satisfaction. Drifting without vision.

**GROUP LEADERS NEED TO RECOGNIZE THAT IT IS NOT THEIR
RESPONSIBILITY TO DELIVER ALL SEVEN ASPECTS OF GROUP LIFE,
BUT IT IS THEIR DUTY TO SEE THAT ALL SEVEN ASPECTS ARE PRO-
VIDED WITHIN THE GROUP.**

Please take some time now to consider the implications of this chapter through the following questions:

1. Which of the seven verbs do you naturally deliver? You may select no more than three.

_____   _____   _____

2. Which do you find more difficult to provide? You must choose at least one and again a maximum of three.

_____   _____   _____

3. Which member in your group best provides in these areas which are not your preference?

_____   _____   _____

4. Consider each member of the group individually and identify the verb you most associate with each person.

Name: Verb:

_____   _____

_____   _____

_____   _____

_____   _____

_____   _____

_____   _____

Chapter **3** *Caring through Small Groups*

From the point of view of members, one measure of the effectiveness of any church structure will be the provision of pastoral care. If we all wrote down our definition of pastoral care, I suspect that there would be considerable differences, but we would know when we deemed the outcome to have felt good! Given the variations in the interpretation of terminology, it is important to go back to Scripture. It is both useful and necessary for us to look at the overall emphasis of the Bible about a particular topic rather than just to squeeze one isolated passage for all its worth. Trying to look at the full picture, I believe that a flawed concept of pastoral care has been propagated that does not really reflect the balance of the New Testament. The first model that usually comes to mind when thinking of pastoral care is the image of the shepherd with the flock, a very comfortable and pleasant pastoral picture. But an examination of the balance of Scripture does not substantiate a preference for this interpretation. There are 13 occurrences of the word "shepherd" in the New Testament and most of them clearly refer exclusively to Jesus. (I've listed them at the end of the chapter.) There are very few suggestions that we could also be included as human shepherds; the references in Acts (ch. 20, v. 38) and Jude (v. 12) are the prime exceptions.

The overwhelming weight of evidence is that the pattern of caring within the church should be based on the principle of "one anothering". If there is a shepherd, he has to be looked after by the sheep! There are 57 references containing this phrase in the New Testament; not surprisingly, some of these simply say "Love one another" which is surely the summary of what pastoral care should be. So the ideal scenario is that everybody pastors and everybody is pastored, but not that everybody pastors everybody else! We are called to minister to each other, rather than look to a select few to do all of the caring. Pastoral care has frequently been professionalized when it should naturally be a responsibility taken seriously by us all. As Smail states: "What we can do for ourselves has been taken from us and given back as a package labelled EXPERT USE ONLY." Dr John Stott warmed to a similar theme at Keswick, saying, "There are too many [leaders] who behave as though they believe not in a priesthood of all believers but in the papacy of all pastors."

Does this conflict with Paul's assertion in Ephesians 4:11–12 about the ministry of a pastor? ("It was he who gave some to be apostles, some to be prophets, some to be evangelists, and some to be pastors and teachers, to prepare God's people for works of service.") No! Although we are all called to provide care, some people are specifically gifted in this ministry. The passion of a mature ministry is in part about expressing that gift, but also about equipping the saints to do similar works of ministry. There is no contradiction between these specialist ministries and the principle of "one anothering". The real pastor is not the minister, elder or leader who behaves like an ultra-busy social worker, but rather a person who recognizes the potential pastor in others, and by a variety of methods, nurtures the tender inexperienced gift to become an effective serving ministry. Many a growing church has had a season of setbacks when one person tries to do all the visiting and caring, sometimes based on an incomplete understanding of these well-known verses that I have quoted above. Dr David Cho (formerly Paul Yonggi Cho) attributes his breakdown in 1964 to trying to do it all himself. (Written up in Chapter 1 of *Successful Home Cell Groups*.)

Many years ago, "Net Contributors" was the title of one of my first sermons. The idea has shed some light to quite a few churches on how "one anothering" should work in practice. All of us, leaders as well as members, need to be receivers throughout our lives. Any other stance would be very unreal. But we need to help some people move from having the mentality of being a net receiver to that of being a net contributor. If we all wanted to principally receive from church life, rather than to contribute, then there would be a shortfall in the available resources. If we think of hospitality, listening, encouragement, giving, comforting, etc., as pots of resource, we need on balance to have more contributions than withdrawals for each and every pot. Better than that, we want sufficient resources to overflow, so that when outsiders are attracted to our lifestyle and want to come and join us, there will be an ample supply to meet their hopes and needs.

The biggest hindrance to developing the mentality of net contributors often appears to be a wrong concept of both the church and full-time ministries. It is as though there is a level of church between the members and God, created to do them good and supply their needs. In reality there is no such tier; we are the church. The Bible teaches us about the priesthood of all believers and there is no basis for looking to a limited number of people to serve the needs of the many, although we are all gifted in certain areas and ministries.

Why has this comfortable but one-sided picture of the shepherd and the flock endured so well? The reasons are probably very complex, but a couple of comments emphasize the problem. Many churches have certainly been doing pastoral care this way for many years so the mentality is thoroughly ingrained. Congregations have learned this way of doing things to such an extent that now they presume that it must be the right way, the only way. It has also suited many ministers and church leaders who want to keep busy and feel needed. And with the pressures on time management in modern life, many members have been too passive to challenge the convenience of the status quo, which provides but does not demand.

Small groups make two contributions towards rectifying the old stereotype. We have already said that everybody should be pastored and in time we should all expect to do some pastoring. There is the potential for chaos here and just as important, the danger that in total informality, some people would inadvertently be missed out.

THE SMALL GROUP PROVIDES THE MINIMUM STRUCTURE FOR THE FIRST LEVEL OF PASTORAL CARE.

The group meeting and the associated friendships should provide a secure opportunity to share needs, pray for each other and provide practical assistance. To emphasize this expectation, in quite a few churches there is an unwritten contract of pastoral care: there is no formal provision of care if you are not a member of a small group. Many pastoral issues may eventually require additional, specialist help but the small group forum is the first port of call and the filter for deciding which issues warrant the time of a more experienced pastor.

There has been some research done about the action church members took when they recognized that they needed help beyond their own "resources". The outcome was:

3% went the formal route, using the systems (and people) provided by the church.
45% sought informal help from friends.
39% sought a combination of formal and informal help.
13% did not seek help at all.

Presumably the middle bands, comprising 84% of the survey, sought out people that they trusted and probably thought of as friends. The small group provides an opportunity to build such friendships in a way that no other aspect of formal church life can deliver, as we have already seen in Chapter 1. Any meaningful level of pastoral care must be based on respect at the very least, and probably the deeper qualities of trust and friendship.

In 1 Thessalonians 2:8, Paul talks about an experience that was very precious to him. "We loved you so much that we were delighted to share with you not only the gospel of God *but our lives as well*" (my italics). This seems to be what the apostle is urging us to work towards. Some care will take place in the group meeting, but far more will have to take place in other situations. In Romans 12:4–5, Paul talks of a similar level of intimacy and interdependence as he had outlined to the Thessalonians: "Just as each of us has one body with many members, and these members do not all have the same function, so in Christ we who are many form one body and *each member belongs to all the others*" (my italics). The idea that we all belong to one another depicts a depth of relationship beyond most of our experiences, with the exception of marriage. The quality of "one anothering" must be largely measured by the interaction of the members outside the evening meeting, not just by looking at a couple of hours of the week in a formal context. The wider community expression will be a better gauge of what we believe and value, not the theology we proclaim.

Obviously when we consider how we should understand "pastoral care" and practise it, there is the temptation to let the expectations of others be the driving factor. The desire to please is very strong. These expectations are likely to be, at least in some measure, unbiblical, incomplete or at worst, downright selfish. It may help to encourage people to see pastoral care at two quite distinct levels. On the one hand, pastoral care can be seen essentially as crisis management, a sort of emergency service that swings into action like a well-trained paramedic unit. Here is an illustration. In the rough and tumble of the playground at school, a six-year-old boy, son of a member of the group, has fallen and broken his arm. While mum dashes from work to the hospital, supportive members of the group pick up her other children when school ends for the day and look after them until mum returns home from the fracture clinic. Perhaps a different member responds by preparing the evening meal for the family. This is a very legitimate example of "one anothering". However, behind this simple story lies a culture of high communication levels, ownership, belonging and responsibility. In recent times in my own local church, quite a few members have had major surgery and have been really blessed and encouraged by the sustained and genuine support from other members, sometimes lasting over a period of months. Quite obviously, in case any of you are still clinging to the mentality of just a few shepherds, it's just not possible for this level of provision to be provided to the whole church by the full-time ministers. (By the way, when I use the term "minister", I mean the "salaried" members, not people who are 7 days a week, 24 hours a day on call.)

The second concept of pastoral care is essentially a longer-term approach and revolves more around development than maintenance. Here are a few New Testament passages that illustrate the essence, which could be called discipling, nurturing or maturing.

Ephesians 4:13 — "Until we all reach unity in the faith and in the knowledge of the Son of God and become mature, attaining to the whole measure of the fullness of Christ."

Colossians 4:12 — "He is always wrestling in prayer for you, that you may stand firm in all the will of God, mature and fully assured."

1 Timothy 4:16 — "Watch your life and doctrine

closely. Persevere in them, because if you do, you will save both yourself and your hearers."

The prime and ultimate responsibility for maturing in Christ is one's own, but in addition to prayer and Bible study, we all sometimes need the insight and support of other people. Indeed some folk can only learn from an interactive approach.

THE SMALL-GROUP SETTING NEEDS TO GIVE BOTH LEVELS OF PASTORAL CARE, THAT IS CRISIS MANAGEMENT AND DEVELOPMENTAL DISCIPLESHIP.

I want to expand on the New Testament concept of the body of Christ and look at a parallel from a completely different field. A few years ago, after communication difficulties in a multi-national oil company, some research into the components of national cultures was undertaken by Gert Hofstede. It was found that cultures would exhibit definable features on four particular dimensions. Whatever the other distinguishing hallmarks of a culture, a measure of these four dimensions was found to be significant. One scale scored the culture of countries on an "independence to interdependence" continuum. The UK score was heavily towards independence and is probably still moving further in that direction. Our culture places a very low premium on community life and corporate responsibility. Those people who have resources and can give support to others are not encouraged in the socialization process to enjoy the privilege of doing so. Many of the implications from the research into national cultures are equally applicable to the culture of churches and other organizations. (We will look at this in more detail in Chapter 8.) I believe that for the church to be effective in taking the gospel to the world, we must clearly exhibit interdependence, in radical contrast to most people's everyday experience. It should be one of our distinguishing features, characterizing the way we go about things. The small group is the most likely forum for us to begin to model and experience this contrast to the world's thinking on a scale which will truly make an impact.

Let's finish this chapter by looking at the weight of biblical evidence. In my concordance, (which may not be the same as yours!) there are 57 references to "One anothering". I want to group them according to the seven verbs from the previous chapter:

JOINING

Accept *one another*	Romans 15:7
Greet *one another* with a holy kiss	Romans 16:16
Greet *one another* with a holy kiss	1 Corinthians 16:20
Greet *one another* with a holy kiss	2 Corinthians 13:12
Greet *one another* with a kiss of love	1 Peter 5:14

HOLDING

Be at peace with *each other*	Mark 9:50
Wash *one another*'s feet	John 13:14
Stop passing judgement on *one another*	Romans 14:13
Together to eat, wait for *each other*	1 Corinthians 11:33
Not become conceited, provoking and envying *each other*	Galatians 5:26
Don't lie to *each other*	Colossians 3:9
Do not slander *one another*	James 4:11
Don't grumble against *each other*	James 5:9

SUPPORTING

Be devoted to *one another*	Romans 12:10
Honour *one another*	Romans 12:10
Live in harmony with *one another*	Romans 12:16
Agree with *one another*	1 Corinthians 1:10
Be patient, bearing with *one another*	Ephesians 4:2

Be kind and compassionate to one
    another, forgiving *each other*   Ephesians 4:32
Forgive, bear with *each other*   Colossians 3:13
Confess your sins to *each other*   James 5:16
Live in harmony with *one another*   1 Peter 3:8
We have fellowship with *one another* 1 John 1:7

GROWING
You are competent to instruct *one
    another*   Romans 15:14
Speak to *one another* with psalms,
    etc.   Ephesians 5:19
Submit to *one another*   Ephesians 5:21
Teach and admonish *one another*   Colossians 3:16
Encourage *each other*   1 Thessalonians 4:18
Encourage *one another*   1 Thessalonians 5:11
Encourage *one another* daily   Hebrews 3:13
Spur *one another* on   Hebrews 10:24
Encourage *one another*   Hebrews 10:25

BUILDING
They discussed this with *one another* Mark 8:16
Have equal concern for *each other*
    as parts of a body   1 Corinthians 12:25
Build *each other* up   1 Thessalonians 5:11

LOVING
Love *one another*   John 13:34
Love *one another*   John 13:35
Love *each other*   John 15:12
Love *each other*   John 15:17
Love *one another*   Romans 13:8
Make your love increase and
    overflow for *each other*   1 Thessalonians 3:12
Love *each other*   1 Thessalonians 4:9
Keep on loving *each other*   Hebrews 13:1

Love *one another* deeply from the heart	1 Peter 1:22
Love *each other* deeply	1 Peter 4:8
Love *one another*	1 John 3:11
Love *one another*	1 John 3:23
Love *one another*	1 John 4:7
Love *one another*	1 John 4:11
Love *one another*	1 John 4:12
Love *one another*	2 John 1:5

WORKING

Serve *one another* in love	Galatians 5:13
Carry *each other*'s burdens	Galatians 6:2
Pray for *each other*	James 5:16
Offer hospitality to *one another* without grumbling	1 Peter 4:9
Serve *others* with (spiritual) gifts received	1 Peter 4:10
Humility towards *one another*	1 Peter 5:5

Contrast this weight of evidence with the 13 references to shepherds:

a ruler who will be the *shepherd* of my people Israel	Matthew 2:6
like sheep without a *shepherd*	Matthew 9:36
I will strike the *shepherd*, and the flock will be scattered	Matthew 26:31
And there were *shepherds*... keeping watch	Luke 2:8
I am the good *shepherd*	John 10:11
I am the good *shepherd*	John 10:14
there will be one flock and one *shepherd*	John 10:16
Be *shepherds* of the church of God	Acts 20:28

Jesus, the great *Shepherd* of the sheep	Hebrews 13:20
returned to the *Shepherd* and Overseer of your souls	1 Peter 2:25
when the *Chief Shepherd* appears	1 Peter 5:4
These men...*shepherds* who feed only themselves	Jude 12
the Lamb at the centre of the throne will be their *shepherd*	Revelation 7:17

The conclusions of this chapter are:

1. There are two valid levels of pastoral care, crisis management and nurture.
2. Pastoral care is the responsibility of the whole flock, encouraged by those with particular gifts of caring.
3. The small group is the natural forum for encouraging and living the principles of "one anothering", that is mutual care and support based on the foundation of an intimate community.
4. There is no difference between cells and other small-group structures in their suitability for this purpose.

Chapter **4** *The Qualities of a Good Small-group Leader*

You might be amazed at some of the statistics about recruitment and selection that the secular world uses as their guidelines. For example, it is not unusual to spend a figure equivalent to the annual salary in order to get the right person, that is to say, if you want the right person for a £50,000-a-year job, then be prepared to spend up to £50,000 recruiting and selecting them. Admittedly, that might include national advertizing, an agency fee and removal expenses. At the other end of the scale, I know a company who will not offer a job to a male applicant who wears white socks to an interview! When I challenged the validity of this method of screening, they would not change their internal and unwritten policy; they were pleased with the general calibre of their appointments and had no impetus to change. After all, as they pointed out, the disciples never wore white socks!

These two illustrations are driven by the recognition of a frequently quoted maxim: the highest cost is the cost of a bad appointment. I want us to apply a little science as well as some divine guidance to appointing small-group leaders, since the cost of a poor appointment can be very high; the growth of God's people can be hampered. The steps in appointing people to a company have further strong parallels in selecting small-group leaders:

1. Write the *job description*

We need to be clear about the task of leading a small group in any particular church. Chapters 5 and 7 will have some useful additional information, but it really is necessary to write a brief job description before we think about the selection criteria used to identify good leaders. Let's take two obvious extremes for illustration. If the small group is principally for Bible study, and the church wants the leader to lecture for the bulk of the time, then the qualities will be very different from a cell leader, whose main role might be the delegation of tasks to other people. There are some major differences between the core requirements of a cell leader and the leadership of other types of groups, as we shall see later.

2. Write the *person specification*

Describe the type of person you would like to appoint as vividly as possible, like a police "identikit". We might need to think about summarizing the information under the following headings:

> Experience
> Knowledge
> Skills
> Values
> Availability
> Personal qualities.

3. Devise and carry out a *selection process*

Not many churches use a formal interview as part of the process of appointing leaders of small groups. That's good; it is a notoriously unreliable tool. Interviews must be designed to elicit information about the criteria that were outlined in the person specification; if we can find those answers in more reliable, practical ways, so much the better.

We need to bear in mind the difference between the

essential features and the *desirable* ones. I suggest that in recruiting small-group leaders, the first three criteria (experience, knowledge and skills) are the least important. If we deem that one of these features is lacking, we can do something about the problem relatively easily. A lack of skill may delay leadership opportunities; weaknesses in personal qualities may prevent selection.

Experience
Previous experience is certainly not essential; leading a small group is a wonderful growth opportunity. Everybody has to start somewhere!

Knowledge
If some knowledge is deemed a core requirement, then the solution simply involves learning, but I cannot imagine a "block" of vital knowledge that is considered necessary for leading a small group.

Skills
Skills can be worked on and improved. We can provide training and coaching designed to meet that shortfall. The small-group context is classically convenient for the "on-the-job" approach to learning. But remember that people have different levels of ability when it comes to skill acquisition, and varying levels of desire to learn particular skills. For example, it is not difficult to train people to ask more and better questions; but if a potential leader doesn't want to do so, then they probably will cease to ask questions in an appropriate manner when the supervision is less intense. A basic level is necessary in each of these skills:

Generating discussion
Asking questions
Listening
Summarizing

Sharing decision-making
Delegation of administrative detail
Forward planning
Resolving conflict
Evaluation.

In later chapters, we consider how to enhance these skills.

Values

I have analysed the subject of values comprehensively in Chapter 8 and the material that we are thinking about here must be thought of in conjunction with the contents of that chapter. A few words of advance notice, stressing the critical nature of this topic will not go amiss. The character and culture of a small group will be substantially influenced by the personal values of the group leader. Therefore, it is absolutely vital that the attitudes projected in the midweek meeting are consistent with the values emanating from the larger church gathering. This consistency is central to church cohesion; we require unity not just in what we do but in the underpinning values, approach and rationale. Trust your discernment in this area; if you have reservations about a potential leader but you cannot focus and articulate them, trust your "gut feeling" and hold back on making an appointment. People with similar values will see church in a similar way. Are they particularly committed to the central position of small groups in the church programme and ethos? That's the acid test.

Availability

The price of leading a small group is often paid principally in hours, not finance or even in emotional costs. We must be open and realistic about our expectations at the outset, especially if the job description requires some pastoral work in addition to the formal meeting time. Remember that often the people we are considering for church leadership positions are also on a legitimate career path and may have young families. If people make themselves unavailable at certain periods of their lives as they balance these priorities, please don't assume that they are uncommitted. Fortunately there are some constructive steps that we can take to alleviate the time management problem. The pastoral demands in different groups will vary and to some extent these variations are predictable. It might be possible to give a less demanding group to a particularly busy leader, so that the additional pastoral hours outside the evening meetings are kept to an acceptable level. There will always be grey areas of pastoral care that can be dealt with either by the group leader or by other people; we can shift that boundary to meet circumstances. Above all, we must not make small group leadership the equivalent of a life sentence; it ought to be possible to serve in this way for a few years and then have a breather or serve in an alternative capacity.

The personal qualities of a small-group leader

We need to be careful that we don't make the entry qualifications so high that St Paul himself would fail to qualify! Often the most effective group leaders are concerned about their inadequacies in the role and don't feel up to the task. Obviously all the qualities of a Christian leader will be found by looking at the person of Jesus as described in the Gospels. That's the source of our standards, but again, be aware of the danger of excluding people who don't measure up to his unique standards.

THE TASK OF A LEADER IS NOT TO MEASURE UP BUT TO GROW UP AND HELP OTHERS TO GROW UP.

In industry and commerce there is a maxim: "Never appoint an over-qualified person." Why is this true?

Because the person will soon get bored. You'll get much better results if there is some challenge in the job. Over the last thirteen years I've worked regularly in one particular Christian conference centre and seen four chefs come and then move on. The best-qualified person had worked in a prestigious hotel and his first weekend task was to cook "bangers and mash" for sixty teenagers! Not surprisingly and by choice, his tenure was the shortest. The ideal chef proved to be a young man who started with the least qualifications and experience. His menus and quality just continued to improve, he went on day-release courses to enhance his qualifications and incidentally became a Christian and found a wife! Inevitably, he moved to a bigger challenge after about seven years; his departure was tinged with sadness and yet the knowledge that the centre had played a significant part in his growth. We need the same attitude in selecting small-group leaders. Many senior pastors are over-protective of the flock and become ultra cautious; the flock do not mind honest mistakes.

I have distilled the key leadership qualities down to ten headings and they are in no particular order of priority. Earlier, I said that you might want to split this list into essential and desirable qualities. I suspect that for some readers all of this list would be deemed essential; it's a matter of degree and the levels that we regard as acceptable. The ten qualities are:

1. Integrity

There are many facets to integrity, yet it is a principal characteristic of trustworthy people. We should be looking for aspects like transparency, people devoid of political manoeuvring and hidden agendas. It would be ideal if other people could say, "What you see is what there is." It's not always necessary to carry your heart on your sleeve, but you must be capable of putting your heart on your sleeve. We have already said that real relationships must involve exchanges at the deeper level of feelings and interpretation, not just facts and the mundane aspects of everyday life. Good leaders want to be known and understood, warts and all.

2. Consistency

Hebrews 13:7–8 makes an open testimonial to a quality of leadership and parallels their leaders with Jesus: "Remember your leaders, who spoke the word of God to you. Consider the outcome of their way of life and imitate their faith. Jesus Christ is the same yesterday and today and for ever."

One of the marks of a mature Christian is a consistent walk through life, not being subject to dramatic fluctuations between peaks and troughs. Violent oscillations are the manifestation of being driven by emotional responses to circumstances, rather than relying on the faithful nature of God. It is distinctly unsettling for members if a leader is barely recognizable as the same person from one week to the next.

3. Self-awareness

Some years ago, I recognized a common trait to three people who I regarded as outstandingly successful in their fields. One is a relation and works in the textile industry; the other two people are church leaders. They all have a very clear and accurate self-assessment. Not only that, but their decisions are consistently based on that knowledge. Weaknesses are accepted as a normal part of the human condition; these people do not confuse having failings with being failures. Many Christians have a tendency to mark themselves down, because they don't want to be seen as arrogant. Unreal self-debasement is no better than arrogance as a reflection of the work of redemption.

4. Positive

The old army joke goes like this:

> Officer: "Let's have an attitude check."
> Private: "I hate this job."
> Officer: "Let's have a positive attitude check."
> Private: "I positively hate this job!"

Hopefully, in contrast, church leaders are essentially optimistic people — they assume that things can be improved. Their view of life is based on "the cup is half full" not "the cup is half empty". Too often the more negative standpoint is characterized by cynicism and listeners easily take a comment on a situation as a reflection on them personally. There is a subtle link here with faith; you have to be an optimistic person to exercise faith. I'm not stereotyping how the exercise of faith should be manifest, neither am I proposing that faith is blind, but the exercise of faith is based on an expectation that the outcome will be an improvement.

5. Passionate

In Revelation 3:16, the initial criticism of the Laodicean church was that it was lukewarm. We might have expected that stone cold would be a worse condition, but evidently not. Leaders need to be passionate people, desperately wanting the best for others and the church in general. Passionate people also hurt, because they care so much, which contributes to a necessary and acceptable vulnerability. Above all, we want leaders who are passionate for Jesus, striving to further that relationship with him above all else.

6. Progressing

During training courses that I am involved in, I have been privileged to share the platform with some memorable speakers. Over the course of the last fifteen years in this work, just occasionally, I have worked with people who are peddling the same materials a decade after I first met them. The cutting edge of their effectiveness just disappears. Their seminars become "dead right", absolutely correct but without life. The same danger exists for leaders of small groups, but from week to week it may prove harder for anybody to spot the downward trend. If a leader is bordering on stagnation in their own life, the cost to the group is very serious, because personal development will cease to be part of the group agenda and culture. I would mark the evidence of consistent progress, as opposed to long static periods, as an essential quality of a group leader. To put it into mathematical language, in many ways the gradient is more important than the height on the graph.

A key indicator for continuous progress is the ability to look constructively at criticism. The leader needs to be able to filter the language in which criticism is delivered in order to analyse the content for accurate substance. People who make progress and help others to grow as well are able to learn from experiences, good and bad. Defensive leaders generally blame other people and miss the learning opportunities inherent in valid feedback. The quality movement in Japanese industry has a concept covered by a single word in their language, for which we have no absolute equivalent in English. *Kaizan* is best translated as "continuous improvement" and that's a mentality that I look for in future leaders. Don't expect them to be perfect but make your expectations of consistent progress very clear indeed.

7. People orientation

Douglas McGregor's frequently quoted theory reckons that the leader's assumptions about people will be reflected in their leadership style. The Theory X leader and the Theory Y leader have contrasting ideas in their assumptions about the nature of people. The following table contrasts the two approaches:

THEORY X LEADERS Assume people generally:	THEORY Y LEADERS Assume people generally:
Lack integrity.	Have integrity.
Are fundamentally lazy and desire to do as little work as possible.	Will work hard towards targets which have their commitment.
Shirk responsibility.	Will accept responsibility within their own sphere and go on to seek more of it.
Need external threat and control for results.	Prefer intrinsic motivation based on fulfilment.
Are incapable of directing their own behaviour.	Are capable of directing their own behaviour.
Are not primarily concerned about the church needs.	Want their church to do very well.
Are not creative.	Have imagination, ingenuity and creativity.

To polarize and stereotype these approaches a bit more, Theory X leaders see their responsibility as organizing the jobs of others since they are incapable or unwilling to organize themselves. They feel that they are required to plan, direct, motivate and control their team members' actions, since without this intervention, members would be passive, even resistant, to the needs of the church. The climate that they produce is authoritarian, mechanistic and coercive; communication is largely in one direction.

On the other hand, Theory Y leaders believe that it is the leader's responsibility to organize the elements of activity, money, resources, equipment and people in order to enable members to do a good job. People are not by nature passive or resistant to organizational needs. They have become so as a result of negative experience and this can readily be changed. Motivation, the potential for development, the capacity for assuming responsibility and the readiness to direct behaviour towards organizational goals are all present in people. Leaders need to make it possible for people to engage their own drives. Theory Y leaders seek to produce a climate that is adaptive, organic, collaborative and open in communication. (In a recent survey of 500 UK companies, 62% reported their management culture to be more X than Y!)

Applying this theory to small groups yields another key quality. Expect strong evidence of a Theory Y approach and the desire to produce an appropriate climate. Look and listen carefully to find indicators about a potential leader's attitude to other people. Not only must they be "growing" themselves, but also they must have that same expectation and hope for their members.

8. Relational

The main functions of leadership revolve around the ability to influence other people. That requires solid relationships. I think that we almost need to be looking at this feature as an attitude rather than a skill. Does the potential leader truly want to build relationships? How are they forged? Are they sustained? What is the basis for the bonding? I look for warmth and a sense of humour. In cell churches particularly, one further evidence of the desire for relationships should be hospitality; it's a vital quality to get the job done.

9. Pure motives

I have read and heard many expositions about leadership and the associated qualities; probably the most common requirement has been the demand for pure motives. This is a difficult thing to discuss simply at the theoretical level; how do we know if a person's motives are pure? It is always more practical to consider the fruits as evidence for the motives.

WE CAN ONLY SEE WHAT PEOPLE DO; WE CANNOT SEE WHY THEY DO IT.

Two additional observations may help our thinking. First, I doubt whether any of us is driven at any time by completely pure motives. I used to query my motives when I was a schoolteacher; did I drag pupils kicking and screaming through external maths qualifications for my benefit or theirs? I never found a completely satisfactory answer. Sometimes I now question the long hours that are demanded of me in order to keep playing league cricket. I'd like to think that one of my reasons for playing is the evangelism at the club, but this just might be an excuse, not a reason! I think that it is good to keep challenging the purity of our motives and to stay sensitive to the conviction of the Spirit. But if we wait until motives are perfect, then we will be desperately short of leaders!

The concept of servant leadership has been much in vogue in the last two decades, probably more at a theoretical level than practical. Servant leaders must still lead; it's how they do it where the difference should be meaningful. Melchizadek is an interesting example of a servant leader. He is only referred to in Genesis 14:18–20, Psalm 110: 4 and Hebrews 7. He was the only Old Testament character to combine the functions of monarch and priest; servant leadership in Christ should combine those elements today.

10. Wise in their use of authority

Jesus was under the authority of the Father and we also need to be respectful of authority before we wield it. How a member responds to authority is an interesting indicator of their leadership potential. Wisdom in the use of authority is probably an issue for us to consider progressively with a small-group leader, rather than to treat it as a core criterion at the outset. Leading the group may well be the first opportunity for the exercise of authority and we cannot expect great wisdom initially. I would, however, expect that clear evidence of the harsh use of authority might prove a serious obstacle to an appointment; negative evidence is very different from lack of evidence.

One or two additional comments need to be made from the experience of cell churches. The senior ministers in the church will appoint cell leaders as the new structure is being adopted. After that stage, the responsibility of selecting and preparing more cell leaders lies with the current cell leader and the zone pastor. Potential leaders are observed over many hours as they take increasing responsibility within the group. Leadership development is vital and so the identification, selection and appointment of cell leaders is a core function within the structure.

Summary
1. The job description of a group leader in your church must drive the person specification.
2. Don't make the entry qualifications for small-group leadership too high; look for increasing evidence of each criterion.

Chapter 5   *Preparing More Group Leaders*

An intern is the relatively new title for a person being trained within a cell to lead a cell in the future. In some respects, there is nothing new about this apprenticeship model other than that it has recently been emphasized by cell churches. We always should have been developing the next cohort of small-group leaders. There was nothing in previous structures to prevent this training happening and the practice ought to have been more prolific. Now we have not only given these apprentices a smart title, but additionally, their training is much more formalized and overtly a very high priority. In the rest of this chapter I will continue to use the "intern" terminology although all of the content is equally applicable to other small-group approaches.

Many people leading cell churches have told me that the cell structure has placed an additional numerical demand on them of finding enough group leaders, especially during the transition period from homegroups to cell church. I believe that these observations have not only been accurate, but the shortfall in numbers will remain and become a more acute problem if the existing small-group leaders do not shoulder their share of the responsibility by seeking out and training interns. If there is one single expectation of cells, it is that they should multiply, and so we need an absolute minimum of one intern per group. Not only must we prepare for growth, but we need to allow for "natural wastage" — people moving away from the area, people being released to a zone pastoral role, and some people needing a legitimate break having served as a group leader for a prolonged season of their life. Inevitably there will also be a few failures as a result of poor selection, preparation and training.

Let's start to look at the training of interns with one important comment about discipleship in general and leadership development in particular. People need more than one "input" contributing to this process. I cannot imagine a scenario where one person can offer all the help in developing character, gift, knowledge and skills that another disciple seeks. Generally people need the exposure to different approaches and styles; anything else is insufficient and potentially dangerous.

"Plans fail for lack of counsel, but with many advisers they succeed" (Proverbs 15:22).

An intern may well receive discipleship from their existing cell leader, the eldership (or equivalent) and a personal mentor or coach. We need to make sure that there is a co-ordinated approach so that each contributor to the training knows what life change they are trying to produce. Good communication is vital to ensure cohesion.

Not only do we need to be clear about the purpose of each training component, but we also must remember that there are many delivery methods. Here are some of the ways that I have seen used, with some possible comments about their application:

APPROACH	POSSIBLE ADVANTAGES	POSSIBLE DISADVANTAGES
External training events	Objective	Not always relevant
Internal training events	Cheaper and focused	Perceived other agendas
Reading	Easy to revisit	Can be dull or not understood
Formal study with qualifications	Portable end product	Slow
Coaching	Skills acquired	Labour intensive
Giving feedback	Close to the event	Needs some trust
Involvement in projects	Learning through experience	Not many options available
Goal-setting and review	Good links to job	Handling failure is important
Delegated tasks	Easily set up	High risk if truly developmental
Exposure to senior decision-making	Not a permanent promotion	Confidentiality issues
Mentoring	Sustained relationships	Are the results fast enough?
Listening to tapes	Done while travelling	No visual impact
Watching videos	Many issues in a short time	Often unreal scenarios
Distance-learning packages	Thorough	Can take years
Lectures	Face-to-face communication	Often too passive
Role-play	Fun!	Might feel too exposed
Simulations	Good for skills	Takes time, incomplete data
Reflection	Looks at the big picture	Not for activist learners
Questionnaire-type instruments	Useful information	Dependent on self-perception

I have insufficient space to amplify each of these methods of learning; suffice to say that they are all very different. I have included the full list to encourage you to look for creative ways of training interns. Let's remember that different people learn in different ways. To some extent, you will be driven in your choice of methods by your own preferences, but the over-riding consideration should be how the intern learns best. I am concerned that training in the Christian sector usually means lecturing, although often with very full notes. The materials available for cell churches have added new dimensions to training and utilized a wider range of delivery methods. There has also been a rediscovery that effective discipleship is very labour intensive because so much of it needs to be conducted on a one-to-one basis. (See Paul and Timothy, Elijah and Elisha, etc.)

Training within the group

There is no better situation to use the principles of coaching than training interns in a small group. The classic pattern is:

I do, you observe
I do, you assist
You do, I observe and assist
You do, I watch
You do, and train more people.

Initially, the intern can try individual components within the evening meeting; invite them to lead any of the ice-breakers, the prayer time, or the study section. Give them as much notice as possible and ask them to contact you after they have done their preparation. Ask questions about their proposals to encourage them to fully consider the implications of their plans. Generally though, don't try to influence their suggestions too much. The danger is that you try to make their sessions too much like your own, and they also need to learn to live with the consequences of their decisions and actions. As the coach, have a chat with the intern after the event, encourage them, and jointly review their contribution to explore ideas for further improvement. Too often, training has involved only the experience, and not been given that little extra time demanded in review. Over a period, you can increase their involvement on a few evenings. After all, the object is to train them to a level where they can lead their own group and at the very least in all types of church structure, that involves co-ordinating or leading a full meeting. It's one thing to lead part of an evening and quite another to experience the full burden of responsibility.

Depending on the mandate of group leaders within your church, the intern may also need to undertake some pastoral responsibilities, making contact with group members, people who have been ill or away, and even prospective new group members. Sometimes this will involve visits, sometimes phone calls. Faithfulness in these aspects of ministry is often a better indicator of servant leadership than the more glamorous role of leading in public. We are looking for a real concern for people and reliability in mundane delegated tasks. There should always be the expectation that the intern will be able to develop the same skill levels as the coach, or better. "A student is not above his teacher, but everyone who is fully trained will be like his teacher" (Luke 6:40). But I hope that we will be exploring ways of encouraging the disciple to even greater heights; the ultimate goal of leadership is that other people should go beyond us.

Years ago, an international company welcomed all new senior managers with a present. Waiting for them on their desk on the first morning was a set of Russian dolls; the sort which contain smaller and smaller dolls as you separate the pieces. Inside the smallest doll was a message:

> **"IF YOU PERPETUALLY APPOINT PEOPLE SMALLER THAN YOURSELF, WE WILL END UP AS A TEAM OF MIDGETS. IF YOU CAN DEVELOP PEOPLE BEYOND YOURSELF, WE WILL END UP AS A TEAM OF GIANTS."**

Let's be very clear about the implications behind this humour: coaching involves the modelling and acquisition of skills. An over-reliance on modelling to the exclusion of other methods of discipleship cannot take others beyond where we are ourselves. We need to be able to help people beyond the limitations of our own competence, especially in areas where we are weak. This cannot be achieved exclusively via modelling. A more varied process of development which includes some less formal opportunities to chat through all sorts of attitudes and issues, including the disciple's personal vision, is to be preferred.

Training from the senior leadership of the church

Apart from the cell leader contributing to the development of the intern, I believe that the senior ministers or elders within the church also have a vital role to play in the development of future group leaders. Currently, when I work with church leaders, I often ask them to respond to two questions as they consider developing new leaders and creating a wider leadership team. The two questions are: "What can best be done with these interns all together?" and "What can only be done by working with them individually?" It makes sense to work with a group when you are addressing common issues, but part of the training process must be personal and therefore unique. These two questions are critical ones for senior pastors to be considering, for the development of the next generation of leadership is one of their prime and non-negotiable responsibilities. Cell principles have increased the focus on the leadership development aspects of discipleship, and are helping to meet a serious shortfall in the life of many churches.

One of the major reasons for the lack of leadership development is the time-management implication for the senior pastor(s). The trouble is that this sort of discipleship is important, but seldom seen to be urgent. "The tyranny of the urgent" phenomenon means that too often priorities are established more on the basis of urgency than importance. Some authors have noted that as a church grows and it has moved to a cell structure, senior leaders have to spend more time with the spiritually "well" and not the "infirm". This is an important change of mentality for senior pastors, and it makes sense to do as much training as possible within a group setting, provided that the content can be made relevant for all those present. Another benefit of group coaching is that the extra dynamics generated by a group are likely to enhance the learning. Sometimes the most effective forum includes the existing small-group leaders as well as those who are being groomed for that responsibility in the future. I strongly recommend that you keep the membership of the training group fluid, despite the appeal of taking a cohesive number through a programme. The bonuses are that you can include borderline candidates and see how they develop in this context, and secondly it minimizes the danger that some people may see an invitation to this group as a status symbol, a step on the "spiritual career ladder".

A training event led by the senior pastors probably includes these components and must be well prepared, with meaty content and value for everybody's time:

> How to affirm and encourage others.
> How to build up the other group leaders and enjoy fellowship with them.
> How to build your faith and the faith of others.
> How to express confidence in God, and lift horizons higher.

How to restate the vision of the wider church, in different ways.

How to emphasize the need for each small group to have a unique vision.

How to maintain a sense of direction, under the corporate umbrella.

How to improve your skills and the skills of others.

How to maintain a perpetual desire for improvement.

How to encourage the on-going identification and training of potential leaders.

How to pray, with people, over them and for them!

How to share our lives as well as our faith.

How to provide a key opportunity for upward communication.

How to learn from each other.

How to say "Thank you".

Visiting other groups as part of intern training

Another form of training that I strongly commend to you is that you encourage, if not actually organize, visits for interns to other groups from time to time. Most interns will have sampled very few small groups in their Christian life; many will have only seen one or two models of leadership, and that's in their present group and church. Wider exposure will broaden their perspective as they experience a range of groups and leadership styles. Even if the group where they are based is generally good, there is always the possibility that "our way" becomes the only right way. Potential leaders obviously get very familiar with one particular style and often don't know how the other groups are operating. As group life progresses from inception to multiplication, so a good leader recognizes the need for a number of different but appropriate approaches. Yet although the approaches can be as different as chalk and cheese, they must remain faithful to the core church values! Spotting evidence of the same core values expressed in groups with different styles can be a great source of encouragement to group leaders and also help provide cohesion in the whole church.

As I have said, visits to other groups can make a very fruitful contribution to a training programme, yet many leaders shy away from providing this opportunity within their church. The usual reason given to me is that a new face will be disruptive to the dynamics of the group that is being visited. That concern may emanate from the hearts of good pastors but actually is not well founded. The visitor should be just that, a visitor, a virtually silent observer, not a contributor. The surprise arrival of a strange member can still have an impact on a group when this first happens, but when such visits become commonplace, then the disruption is minimal.

The training content should be driven by the job description and the individual needs

We need to think about the type of training that would be appropriate for interns in the light of their experience, competence, prior learning, job description and the width of their responsibilities. If the role of the group leader is limited to the organization of a midweek evening meeting, then the essential training is fairly limited. If the mandate is altogether a wider brief and includes a broad pastoral responsibility, then the training needs to be more extensive. We might take this opportunity to train to an even deeper level if the person is seen as a potential zone pastor, without guaranteeing any future role.

We should always be providing two levels of training. The first level is before the intern takes up their position as a group leader, making sure that they have sufficient basic competencies to start the job. Don't underestimate the importance of this level of training; some people who have not lasted the pace and stopped group leadership at a very early stage only needed a little reassurance. Other people suspected that they could do the job, but they still had to be convinced. Additional to this initial training, we need to provide ongoing opportunities, recognizing that learning is a lifestyle and that the provision of such training is part of our commitment to group leaders.

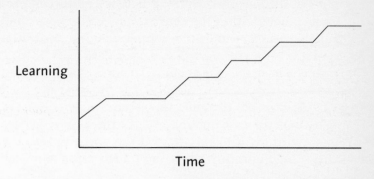

Even for the most enthusiastic learners, there will be plateaux on the growth path when experience is being consolidated. We need to ensure that training has contributed to adequate *preparation* for the demands on people during those plateaux, so that they can cope without undue stress. Training which takes place *after* experience on a plateau will reinforce the knowledge and skills.

Creative options for developing interns

There are additional approaches to training which need cost none of the trainer's time at all. Consider the many things that we do where an intern might accompany us. I know of churches where the leaders have their apprentices with them regularly during their devotional times. In these cases the leaders have recognized that there can be value in sharing their personal walks in Christ. The whole idea of involving other people like this might sound surprising to you and more than a little risky or inhibiting. Correct! It is actually because of the risk and associated vulnerability that the coaching has proved so effective and really has formed the basis of the relationships. Other leaders I know will frequently take an intern with them on pastoral visits. Again, doubts can spring to mind immediately, about things like confidentiality and the ability to get to real issues when a third party is present. None of these concerns is too stifling, provided that there is a culture of people development within the church. How will we ever find out whether people can handle confidential information if we cannot take the initial risk and offer trust?

(Did you hear the joke about the eldership who decided to meet together and share deeply? The first one admitted to being susceptible to drink, the second leader disclosed difficulty in resisting gambling, and the third shared about struggles with his thoughts toward the opposite sex. The meeting closed abruptly when the fourth elder admitted that he was a bit of a gossip!)

Any car journey is also an opportunity to share conversation time, always keeping your eyes on the road, of course! That's just three examples of excellent opportunities for training interns, without changing your own time budget. In all these situations, the testimony has been that the learning process is two-way and certainly keeps the coaches on their metal.

In conclusion

Churches that have adopted cell-church principles have made great strides towards a revolution in training. For many years, perhaps centuries, training for Christian service in the local church focused on knowledge and theology. Skills were virtually not on the agenda. Slowly, there is an emerging climate that skills' training is both necessary and legitimate.

It's hard to define the culture that fosters real personal development, but it is essential for learning and certainly includes:

People taking responsibility for their own actions, ownership not blame.

Working to medium, not short-term, time horizons.

Co-operative not competitive relationships.
Theory-Y management style.

Many companies have shown that, in isolation, a substantial training budget and an appraisal system, although necessary, are not sufficient to ensure personal growth and development. The expectations of their staff have to be changed. The cell-church initiatives have illustrated what can be done when we truly promote training as an integral sub-set of discipleship.

Chapter **6 The Responsibilities of Being a Small-group Leader**

Task, authority and accountability together form the basis of any delegated responsibility. They need to be expressed clearly and be consistent with each other.

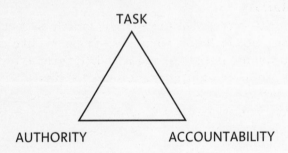

TASK

AUTHORITY   ACCOUNTABILITY

Task

The task is the function that we are asked to undertake, essentially the areas that I have called the job description in previous chapters. One church summarized the role of a small-group leader like this: "To lead, facilitate and equip the members of the group so that together they may fulfil their group mission."

Superficially, that description sounds very fine, but a closer examination reveals its inadequacies. It doesn't say much more than that the group leader's job is to lead, facilitate and equip the group! In practice, and by discussion, we need to tease out clearer boundaries by looking at questions like these:

> Are you being asked to lead the meeting or organize/facilitate it?
>
> What should you be providing outside of the evening meeting?
>
> At what point does your pastoral mandate end, and the work of the senior leaders begin?
>
> What opportunities are within your remit to offer to members as they develop their gifts?
>
> Are you responsible for following up absent members assigned to your group?
>
> Is there a minimum or maximum time expectation of you in leading the group?
>
> What documentation are you expected to maintain?

Authority

Authority is accorded to you, not something that you can impose, especially on volunteers. It's a bit like soap, the more you use it, the less you have left. Secular job descriptions are very careful about defining the limits of authority and they are usually, rightly, expressed by what you should not do. The implication is that any exercise of authority outside these limits is unacceptable, but to the extent of these boundaries, you are expected to take decisions.

I have sometimes found it useful to categorize leaders into two broad types. There are those people whose greater temptation is to under-use their authority. Other leaders are more prone to challenge their boundaries and push them further out, assuming more authority than they have been given. There are many more group leaders in churches from the first category and they are certainly less dangerous in the short term. In the long run however, it is very draining for the senior pastor to find that they are still lumbered with tasks and decisions that they had tried to delegate. It is good to know ourselves well and to recognize our vulnerabilities: to which side of the authority spectrum are you likely to stray?

Put simply, it is neither desirable nor possible to specify the responsibilities or the authority in a way that will cover every contingency. Job descriptions that attempt to do so are very lengthy and soon become obsolete. They focus too much on the present, in great detail, without properly highlighting the principles of the role. The only solution is to maintain excellent communication channels, especially in times when there are pastoral difficulties or possible misunderstandings.

Accountability

We should all want to be held accountable for our leadership of a group. We will be called to account eventually and it is much better to be supported and challenged now. The opposite of being under authority could be entitled "the loose cannon" or "doing your own thing". If we want our leadership to remotely follow the model of Jesus, we must renounce that independent and self-gratifying use of authority. Again, good upward communication is a key characteristic of a leader who wants their group to be properly integrated into the wider church community, and who also wants their use of authority to be appropriate.

When delegation goes wrong, the usual reasons are down to the delegator, not the person entrusted with the job. This may surprise you if your first thought was about unfaithful group members who do not finish what they are asked to do! The single most common reason for failure in a delegated task is that the member, who was given the task, was not given the necessary authority to accomplish it. Neither can we (righteously!) try to hold somebody accountable when we have retained the critical authority level; I'm afraid that in such a situation, it's still our job. It is also wise for both parties to be conscious of the possibility that each person might make false assumptions and leave tasks to the other. Health and safety, financial and child-protection issues are examples where double-checking is better than sorrow.

Your own spiritual health

The greatest responsibility of anyone in leadership is to maintain their own relationship and walk with God. The central theme of the temptations of Jesus (Matthew 4) was the attempt to sever the communication between Jesus and the Father; it is no different for us. We primarily minister out of who we are, not what we have done or learnt. The most important message in this chapter is that in any form of leadership, we have an increased responsibility to be walking in the Holy Spirit. For example, no amount of technical preparation can provide for that sensitive moment, when moved by compassion, we minister in the gifts of the Spirit.

Motives

I believe that as part of our frequent spiritual health checks, we should seriously question our motives for wanting to lead a small group. Increased purity of heart in this area should be part of our sanctification, recognized and evidenced by the fruit of the Spirit. If status is important to us, small-group leadership can be seen as a rung on the ladder; of member, intern, cell leader, zone pastor, elder, full-time staff... international itinerant deliverance minister! Although that pecking order is meant humorously, many churches have quietly propagated a career path mentality. That attitude comes from the world and should have no place in church life (although there is clearly a hierarchy of angels!). The value base is fundamentally different, in that positions of leadership are not for our own edification. The ministry should be sufficiently satisfying in itself, coming from the sure knowledge that it is what God has called us to do at the present time. It is not primarily a stepping stone to a "higher calling". With the privileges of any leadership position also come the responsibilities. If we are not serious about the costs of leadership, we should be prepared to decline the invitation to lead a group.

Sadly, the temptation to focus on status is closely associated with people strongly motivated by an immature desire to influence. It is part and parcel of that personality type, a predictable vulnerability. As we grow in Christ, the temptation will continue to be there, but we can and should learn to handle it better. If we resist the enemy, he will flee from us.

Prayer

Soak your small group in prayer! You know it makes sense! Perhaps we should all take our prayer lives as a measure of how much we value the people in our group. I'm not going to give a great exposition on prayer; it is not the purpose of this book. But at least let's note that Jesus did not focus his prayer life on the unsaved world; prayer for him meant talking with his Father and praying for his disciples (Luke 22:32 and John 17:1,9,15,20, etc.). Even now he intercedes for us! His two principal concerns were his relationship with the Father and his love for those that he was equipping to do the work. If you are short of time, make prayer the priority as opposed to detailed preparation. Both would be wonderful! The leader needs to model the importance of prayer; it can get squeezed out on both the individual and corporate levels.

The contrast between leadership of home groups and leadership in cell churches

The preparation required for each meeting illustrates one of the biggest contrasts between the most traditional type of homegroups (which are often a Bible study) and the cell-church principles. In some ways, leading a cell is far more challenging than leading a homegroup, because the width of expectation is usually wider. If the norm is "multiply or be disbanded", then the bulk of the evangelistic fervour of the church has to be expressed at the small-group level. The role of the cell leader can be particularly demanding in the transition to cells, or if there is still a culture barrier to be surmounted. Adjusting to worshipping in a small group and accepting fresh concepts of discipleship don't happen overnight. It is for these reasons that many people experience that being a leader in a cell church is more difficult than in other structures. The role is more complex and there are more priorities to be juggled; cell church requires very different leadership.

So while the combined responsibilities of leading a cell may be wider, the week-by-week preparation of the meeting can be much less demanding than in historical homegroups. If the main emphasis is on a Bible study, and the onus is on the leader to be a teacher, the research can mean a great deal of preparation to cover the theological background. The worst sort of studies are long on information, and too frequently are short on application, though there is no structural reason for this imbalance. I want to go back to one of the original reasons of this book. It isn't necessary for house groups to be like that, and never was. Roles could always have been delegated, the ministries shared around the members, and the programme could have been very varied.

Preparation

Some of the elements of preparation that are similar in both homegroups and cells might include the list below. It is not the group leader's responsibility to do all of these, but it is their responsibility to see that they are all done.

1. Comfort

The venue needs to set the right ambience for the meeting. Ideally, the room must be large enough to accommodate the members in relative comfort, the temperature neither too cold nor conducive to sleep, and the drinks and biscuits adequate!

2. Communication
Advance notification of meetings in many churches takes little account of the full diaries of today's members. Members deserve the maximum possible notification if there is to be a change of venue, a cancellation of the usual meeting because a guest speaker is in town, an alteration to the regular night of the week, or perhaps a break during the school holidays. Obviously, cancellations don't present major difficulties but too often it is a change to the regular night of the week or extra meetings when the member's commitment is presumed upon. Generally, make sure people are informed about the programme at least twice, once verbally, then by confirming the details in writing, and perhaps also using a communication chain system. Poor communication is very unsettling for all of us, and particularly so for new or fringe members.

3. Content
I do have some criticism of a cell structure where the expectation is that all four "W"s must be done every week. It has been said semi-seriously that each of the four components should have a standard twenty-two-and-a-half minutes per evening. There is a serious point behind this comment. Often the time available for the small-group meeting is about one and a half hours, after calculating time for refreshments at either the beginning or the end of the meeting. That really does mean that most meetings are running to a very tight time schedule, assuming that we want to touch the four "W"s each week. Experience has shown that the way around this difficulty is to allocate the time unequally; "welcome" should be given longer in the early stages of the group's life and "works" have the lion's

share in the later stages. Deciding the time allocation for the different components of the evening is a key part of the leader's preparation. If you have assigned the leadership of each part to different people, they need to be aware of your hopes. Again, the unexpected can happen and it is only sensitivity to the Spirit that should determine whether we stick to the plan, consciously deviate, or call the meeting back to the designed path.

4. Changing lives

Remember that one of the main aims of the small group is to see people grow and develop. So it is important to think about not only the content, or just completing yet another meeting, but about your desired outcomes. What do you want the evening to achieve? Sometimes having a sense of just one or two key lessons for no more than a couple of people would be a satisfactory result. Small specific aspirations, prayerfully targeted, often produce more fruit than a generally aimed programme. Single meetings seldom produce major life changes by themselves, but I don't think it is necessarily wrong to focus on a couple of individuals, either in the content or in your prayer preparation. Ultimately people are responsible for working out their own salvation, but we still need to be focused in our preparation. If our hope is that every part of the evening blesses everybody, we are in danger of hitting nothing!

IT IS GOOD TO REVISIT YOUR PROJECTED CONTENT AND THINK OF RESULTS, NOT MATERIAL.

5. Check progress

We shall look at evaluation in much more detail in Chapter 14, but the acid test of a good meeting will be whether it achieved the desired outcomes for the evening and how it has contributed to the longer-term vision for the group. Assessing progress against the longer-term vision is hard to discern from one individual meeting to the next, but that is no excuse for avoiding a regular check on the progress.

Your personal development

Being invited and appointed to lead a small group should be the beginning of an exciting learning curve. It shouldn't be interpreted with a sense of "having arrived". However optimistic or frail we may feel in the role, we can and should always improve. The bulk of the later part of this book deals with the skills that are fundamental to small-group leadership. Skills should never be regarded as static, even though they are unlikely to change rapidly. Every small-group leader should have three or four specific steps per year for their own improvement. That really is the right number; the two biggest dangers are that we either try to change the world overnight or finally take no action for development, despite much thought! It will be harder to set goals for your own development in the realm of pastoral care, but it can be done. At the simplest level, an improvement might be that you would telephone all members of your group once per fortnight unless you have spoken to them individually.

We can't go far wrong in leading a small group if we humbly remain more aware of our responsibilities than the privileges. Members will come to understand the attitude in our hearts over a period of time; the messages will come through loud and clear. Are we there to serve God and indirectly therefore to serve them, or for ourselves?

Summary

1. Keep checking your motives.
2. Accept the responsibilities as gladly as the privileges.
3. The root cause of many mediocre meetings is the lack of preparation.
4. The three secrets are prayer, more prayer and praying continually!

Chapter **7**

Clarifying the Small-group Purpose

This chapter, in conjunction with the next two, is designed to help you find the vision for your small group. Vision is a big buzz word, but it is not always used accurately or consistently. I will clarify how I interpret the meaning of the word and show how the concept can be a powerful tool. Vision is certainly not the highest-ranking feature in forward thinking. It is subordinate to purpose and values, which we will therefore look at first. I have never known a meaningful and practical vision emerge, without the purpose and values being clarified first.

Current literature is divided in its choice of language; the words "purpose" and "mission" are often used interchangeably. Probably more authors use the term "mission" than use "purpose". (It's interesting that the wider world is choosing to adopt the language of the church.) I prefer to use the term "purpose" because it describes the concept rather better. We are trying to answer the question "Why does this organization/group exist? What is its raison d'être?" We must consider the purpose of the church universal first, before we can get a meaningful answer at a local congregational level, and hence eventually for a small group as part of the local church. Remember that this chapter is designed as a practical tool, not just as a linguistic exercise. Merely playing with words is not productive.

The answer to the question "What is the purpose of the church universal?" is sometimes reckoned to be either so difficult or alternatively so obvious that the question should not be asked at all! I have had many answers to this question during seminars, but there seem to be a few common components that reflect the balance of Scripture, rather than isolated verses taken out of context. The purpose of the church seems to be primarily fourfold:

Worship

God is worthy of worship by his very character and nature. The church, seen as the bride being made ready for the groom, is drawing together to give him his due praise and glory. Worship has many forms and should be expressed both individually and corporately. In the book of Revelation, there are many verses about worship relating to the age to come, but no references to evangelism, for obvious reasons. Worship is eternal.

Evangelism

Another major thrust of the New Testament is that we are called to take the good news to others. We are instructed, "Therefore go and make disciples of all nations, baptising them in the name of the Father, and of the Son and of the Holy Spirit, and teaching them to obey everything I have commanded you" (Matthew 28:19–20). That brief will continue throughout the life of the church universal.

Discipleship

In the great commission we are instructed to make disciples; we were never instructed to make only converts. There should be an on-going process of learning holiness, as we become more familiar with Jesus' commands. Corporately, this is a further expression of the bride being made ready for the bridegroom. Salvation is only the beginning of the journey.

The body of Christ, a relational community

There are frequent biblical pointers to the dynamic that the body is more than the sum of the parts. We shall look at the whole issue of interdependence in a later chapter. It is sufficient to say for now, members were never designed to function in isolation; we are called to model community to the outside world.

After these four core purposes, individual congregations sometimes include a combination of three more:

Locality

The four functions listed above (worship, evangelism, discipleship and the relational community) are a brief summary of the purpose of the church universal. Structurally and administratively, there needs to be a rationale for subdividing the worldwide church into manageable units. I believe that the overwhelming biblical evidence is for a structure based on the grounds of locality, and not as we have today, denominationally. What are the implications of this principle? Most churches will gladly accept members that choose to travel some considerable distance to meet with them, although I know of one very big church which asked members not to attend their congregation if they needed to drive past another similar church en route to their building. But in terms of our outreach and evangelistic programmes (eg visitation or leaflet delivering), finance and manpower dictate that we target a limited geographical area. Most denominations, especially the parish system in the Anglican and Roman Catholic Church have put in place a structure of sub-division based on locality.

I still find quite a few individual church purpose statements that talk about "to the ends of the Earth", with no lesser limitation on their zone of operation. Usually this type of statement reflects a zeal for outreach and a desire to reach areas of the globe that have not yet been touched by our traditional missionary efforts. Far be it from me to discourage people from the biblical mandate! But the Scriptures do not require all churches to operate in all parts of the world. It's logistically impossible. Individual churches that are sending missionaries need a basis for deciding which areas outside their immediate locality are their priority. A colleague visited a church that had the purpose statement "To see the world saved"! There was consternation when he asked, "Oh, and how are you getting on so far?" I believe that the first mission priority for all churches should be their immediate neighbourhood, and the limits of the focus of your energies is worth defining.

Sending

Many churches have a passion for sending ministries to other parts of the world and perhaps we are recently also recognizing the need to *receive* other ministries as well! No longer is mission purely a "first world sent out to the third world" mentality. Equally, particularly with generation X paradigms, there are many more people using a gap-year or short-term placement to fulfil a missionary call. Early retirements are dramatically on the increase and perhaps there will be more opportunity for "mission after work".

Planting

The most effective way of providing church to a geographical area might be by centralizing people and resources in one large congregation or it may be by planting new churches in the surrounding districts. For constitutional reasons, planting is more difficult in some denominations than in others (for example, there are legal considerations associated with the parish system in the Anglican Church), and certainly it requires greater consultation. But some churches would want to see themselves as a resource, involved in planting additional congregations. There is no doubt that this strategy has resulted in significantly greater attendance overall, in certain towns; both methods are valid.

The small-group meeting is part of the whole church programme and offers an opportunity to fulfil some or all of these purposes. The mandate of the group should be seen in conjunction with the purpose of the remainder of the church programme. In the cell movement, the small group has a dramatically enhanced place within the programme: it is absolutely central! The bigger meeting on a Sunday is an important level of celebration but no longer holds that former unique position. And so it is a general principle that every small group meeting should contain the four "W"s:

Welcome
The word "icebreaker" is frequently used as the basic activity for this stage. Most people arrive at a cell meeting somewhat disorientated and distracted, full of the cares of the day, barely ready to contribute and not focused on building one another up. The purpose of the icebreaker is to gather the hearts and minds of distracted members, ready to work towards the common purposes.

Worship
Worship can be done in a small group as well as at congregational level, but many people find it less comfortable. Creative options include less singing, the use of CDs, more contemplation, prayer and Scripture reading. (See note at the end of this chapter.)

Word
This section often involves some discussion around the previous Sunday sermon, and the application of that teaching to everyday life. The essence of the community life includes helping and supporting each other in those applications.

Works

This is the outreach element where, via mutual support and encouragement, the members are focusing on external friendships and personal evangelism.

It is very important to remember that the four "W"s are not sacred. I have already put forward an alternative in Chapter 2. They are one possible arrangement to help us fulfil the eternal purposes of the church universal. Too often, they have become an answer to "What should we do?" Purpose is deeper and answers the question "Why do we exist?"

Historically, the homegroup meeting has often focused on at best two of the four "W"s, the Word and Works. There was never any fundamental reason why groups could not be asked to meet different purposes, and especially recently, there have been more variations. I have known groups under different titles meeting the friendship and community aspirations of the members. Kinship, Koinonia, Community, and Life Groups are among the range of titles which are accurately reflecting their group's purposes. Some, usually for a more limited duration, are task or project focused. They might centre on the decoration of the building, video distribution or visitation. Alpha courses could be seen as a variation on this theme, especially if you are not expected to retain membership of an additional group simultaneously.

Two other types of group are commonly found and therefore deserve a mention. If overseas mission is seen as important, but support is principally prayer and finance, mission groups can meet with a continental focus, eg the Africa group or the South America group. More frequently, mission groups are based around a particular society and inspired by a few individuals. Many churches still tithe their income to overseas missions, but the heart for overseas work is usually greater if the church has sent people to the field. Rightly, mission group meetings are generally additional to other midweek structures and I don't see a member being part of a missionary group, to the exclusion of a cell or homegroup, as being a good option. The focus of a missionary-group meeting is simply too narrow to meet the full needs of the member.

There is also the question of prayer groups. You may have noticed that prayer was not on my list as one of the core purposes of the church universal, although a very good case could be made for doing so. Prayer can be split under two principal headings at the corporate level: as part of worship and as part of intercession. For now, I am putting prayer primarily under worship. Seeing prayer as a means to an end, as in intercessory prayer for example, rather than as an end in itself is inadequate, but prayer should underpin every other purpose and ministry within the church.

Setting aside the theology of prayer, the more practical issue is the place of corporate prayer in the church diary. Generally, little time is given to prayer within Sunday services. For churches wishing to put greater emphasis on prayer, either there is additional time pressure within the existing small-group meeting or an extra meeting slot has to be found. Often this will be early morning, another midweek evening, or Sunday evening if there is only one main service. Some churches abandon the normal small-group programme for one week each month to create the space for a prayer time. All too frequently, the outcome is that the prayer life of our churches is the poor relation among the other demands on our time.

Your group purpose(s)

Whatever your paradigm and structure, it is vital that the group leader knows why the group exists, what is its purpose and how it integrates with other parts of the church programme. In cell churches, as I have already said, the small group is now central to the life of the church and therefore must reflect all of the church purposes. That cell community is the basic unit of church life, although not all of the purposes are exclusively fulfilled in the context of a group meeting. I personally agree that the small group should be one of the two basic units of church life, along with the "celebration" (the whole congregation) in any structure. This conclusion has major implications for the content of the small-group meeting. But it seems an extra and unnecessary step to require all groups to include the four "W"s in every meeting, even in varying proportions. That stipulation shows a lack of flexibility taking too little account of group size, need and maturity. It seems a legitimate interpretation, for example, to say that the Sunday meeting is largely focused on worship and the word, and that the small group emphasizes other elements of church life, such as evangelism and relationships.

Here then are some of the potential purposes of any small group. Check through the list and tick the ones that are expected of your group and put a cross if this function is not part of your group mandate. If you want to add an additional refinement, assign a priority as well, scoring high, medium and low alongside the features that you have ticked.

Possible purpose	Tick/cross	Priority level
1. Worship	_____	_____
2. Bible study	_____	_____
3. Application of Sunday, or other, teaching	_____	_____
4. Social events	_____	_____
5. Discipleship	_____	_____
6. Training	_____	_____
7. Prayer for each other	_____	_____

8. Prayer for outreach events _____ _____

9. Overseas mission involvement _____ _____

10. Evangelism, initial contact for
new members _____ _____

11. Putting on evangelistic events,
eg Alpha _____ _____

12. Integrating new members _____ _____

13. Multiplication of the cell _____ _____

14. Pastoral care _____ _____

It is important that the expectations of the small group are realistic. Can your present programme meet the high priority ticks in your list? It is not possible to have all of the above as a high priority every week. A typical evening just isn't long enough. Some, certainly, are likely to be achieved naturally if others are deliberately fulfilled. As a group leader, this purpose or mandate is the first thing that must be clearly understood, and if it isn't, please ask your senior pastor for clarification. It is legitimate for the priorities within the above list to shift from month to month or even from week to week. The cell-church movement has demanded a very radical reassessment, rightly recognizing that some aspects of church life have virtually been ignored within the more traditional structures.

Chapters 4 – 6 look at the group leader's personal roles and responsibilities. Remember that this chapter is concerned with the joint purpose of the whole group and not the task of any individual.

(May I commend three CDs by Phil Lawson Johnston, specifically designed for small group worship. They are available direct from the Cloud Trust, 307 Woodstock Road, Oxford OX2 7NY).

Chapter **8**

Consistent Values

I read a book recently about Christian youth work that gave me cause for considerable concern. It asked whether we had any right to teach values, and if we presumed to do so, then which values should we teach in the context of working with impressionable teenagers? For me, the book was well wide of the mark in even asking one of these questions at all; you will unavoidably be teaching your values to others, simply by living! You are a walking, 24-hours-a-day values transmission system! The transmission of values cannot be switched on and off like a neon sign. In everything we do we give messages that exhibit our core values. It's not primarily about what we do but the way that we do it.

Just as we continually model our personal values, so the same principle applies corporately in church life. We need to analyse those corporate values because that's where our distinctiveness probably lies, not in our purpose or functions. It's not that we worship that makes us unique but the manner in which we worship. Ultimately people will join us or not, and stay with us or not, on the basis of these underpinning values.

Let's start by clarifying any potential language difficulties with a definition. Values are principles or beliefs that guide decisions and actions. Values must therefore:

Define the requirements of good relationships.

Focus on how we do things, and how people are treated, and not on what we do.

Be mandatory and therefore a prime responsibility of all in leadership.

Be evidenced in many visible examples of behaviour.

(David Cormack, *Change Directions* [Monarch, 1995].)

Values are not the same as doctrine but they may come out of doctrine. They also come out of other features like culture, upbringing and education. I have been to churches in the Pentecostal denominations and to New Churches that would both describe themselves as "charismatic". Doctrinally they have very few differences and none of substance but often they feel completely different. Anglican churches in neighbouring parishes may apparently have the same thirty-nine articles and even similar styles of worship but have very different values and culture. Suppose the values in church A could be described as accepting, friendly, compassionate, and supportive whilst church B's values could be summarized as passionate, excellent, pioneering and focused. The churches could easily hold identical doctrinal positions and justify their different values from scripture. Yet the churches would certainly feel very different. Values are subordinate to doctrine and values should guide, without "cloning", behaviour.

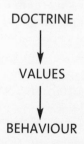

DOCTRINE

↓

VALUES

↓

BEHAVIOUR

The values that we transmit are a matter of choice but they only change slowly. Many people will accept to a large degree what their parents stood for; other people will dramatically reject those values and adopt another set purely because they would want to be different from their parents. Four sets of values are at play in the small-group scenario. There will be the personal values of the group leader, the values of the individual members, the collective common group values and the core values of the umbrella church. The sum of the effect of the core values is called the "corporate culture". About five or six words or short phrases should be sufficient to understand and communicate your culture and therefore something of your uniqueness. If you include too many, the minor ones will neither be evident or remembered. (We need to identify the values before we try to communicate them.) In a group of less than a dozen people, the leader's personal values may come through very strongly, especially if one of the leader's core values is autocracy!

Let me compare two churches that I have been to recently and show you some contrasting messages observed purely in the presentation of the notices. The content is unimportant for this comparison. (See following page.)

Each of these differences is largely meaningless and insignificant in isolation, but newcomers will observe hundreds of these verbal and non-verbal messages during their visit and subconsciously sort them into patterns. So the use of the minister's title and surname may have no significance whatsoever; on the other hand it may be one of many messages that reinforces an impression of a church where status, qualifications or dignity are important. If a message is repeated sufficiently often, then the receiver will draw a conclusion about a core value.

Articulation of the values is part of the process which I use in helping churches right through to finding their vision. Here are the values of two churches, which ought to

CHURCH A	CHURCH B
The contents of the verbal notices were a replica of the written sheet that had been distributed at the door.	The verbal notices were additional to the handouts and more personal to the life of the members.
People were formally referred to by their title and surnames.	People were referred to by their Christian names.
No humour and certainly no laughter.	Humour was used and helped to maintain the concentration of the listeners.
No mention of thanks for members' contributions.	Specific thanks for practical help within the church during the past week.
The notices were read word for word from prepared written notes.	The notices were informal and the speaker was making eye contact at all times.
The notices apparently were always at the same point in the service every week.	The notices apparently appeared at different points in the services from week to week according to their nature and importance.

give you a feel of the sort of statement that can prove useful. One church identified their values as:

1. Passionate for God, his word and the power of his Spirit.
2. Passionate for healthy relationships, family feel and interdependence.
3. Passionate for his people, accepting, compassionate and supportive.
4. Passionate for simplicity and transparency.
5. Passionate for releasing people to their full potential.
6. Passionate for fun and laughter.

Another church produced this set of values:

1. Accessible, biblically based teaching.
2. Warm, welcoming and accepting.
3. Integrity, we will walk the talk.
4. Seven-day-a-week participation.
5. Caring for and encouraging one another and others.
6. Challenging.
7. Joyful.

Values are caught and not taught. The leader's messages within a new group, or to a new member of an existing group, will be very significant. So I am suggesting that the critical requirement in selecting people for group leadership is that they own and attempt to consistently live out the core values of the church. However suitable a potential group leader may otherwise appear, in character or skills, it is of paramount importance that they stand for the same values as the senior leadership in the church. If a new family comes to your church this weekend, it is vital that they see consistency in all the meetings and expressions of the life of the church. Wherever they cut the stick of rock, it must say "Blackpool"! It is very confusing if the Sunday service, the children's work and the midweek group don't transmit the same value messages. Most people don't analyse what is happening to them in a logical way as I have articulated values here. They are very sensitive in picking up the small indicators, yet often the identification of the values is a subconscious process. Having kept their eyes and ears wide open in the excitement of a new experience, they are nevertheless fairly confident about their conclusions when the messages are consistent.

I saw an example of a values difference between leaders in another church that I visited recently. The pastoral approach in the church is very interesting. In general, you would say that the church is God-focused rather than problem-orientated. If you have a "small" problem, just keep rhythmically walking along the path of life. There is a job to be done and there isn't time to stop at the wayside for every little problem. Issues are dealt with as they walk together. (Incidentally, there is real care in this church and when there are major pastoral difficulties, the leaders are incredibly supportive and available.) However, one small-group leader would by nature make his care more obvious for many people with problems and spend more time being manifestly supportive. Certainly he would be prepared to be available to individuals as a very high priority, even to the extent of missing formal church meetings. I leave it to you to decide whether this was merely a style difference or whether the approach to pastoral care should be seen as a difference at the values level. The outcome in this particular church was that the difference was seen as quite fundamental, confusing to members and symbolic of other areas where the individual group leader would not quite be in harmony with the general ethos.

Strangely, good research on teams and small groups seems to happen intermittently; there were major insights in the thirties, sixties and at the end of the seventies in the last century, but also fallow periods with little new in the way of insights. Tuckman's analysis of the stages of group life was finished in 1965 and applies very well to the small group in a church setting. He concluded that groups went through four distinct phases in their life cycle, which I believe reflect a coming together of the values of the group:

A. Forming

At this stage, the group barely deserves to be called a group; it is simply a collection of individuals with very different values. People will react differently, partly based on personality and degree of self-confidence. Some will be very keen to make their mark and establish their identity and individuality. The focus needs to be on the leader at this stage because the values are being moulded. The parallel stage in the Gospels is in the early chapters, where Jesus selected his team and they believed in him (John 2:11). The focus was on the leader, not on the task or the benefits of the group. A bit like the relationships in some homegroups, I'm not convinced that all the disciples actually liked each other! Fortunately, we are not called to like one another, only love one another.

B. Storming

The honeymoon period is over and superficial consensus can collapse. Roles, norms and even leadership can be challenged. Hidden agendas can emerge and there may well be considerable inter-personal conflict. Values underpin every action and decision and during this phase it becomes very apparent that different people want to do most things in different ways. Successful management of this stage is critical if there is to be real trust within the group later. Tuckman suggested that many groups spend well over 50% of their life cycle in these first two stages. Many conflicts that emerge after the honeymoon phase revolve around issues of values and are therefore potentially serious.

C. Norming

Slowly, with much tentative testing, the group will establish its own culture, its own way of doing things, based on an emerging set of common and agreed values. Some people may have left or transferred, but if your group norms are consistent with those of the wider church, there is every possibility that people who want to change groups will encounter some of the same problems in a parallel group. At this stage, different people will manifest different levels of commitment.

D. Performing

Most groups will achieve some measure of success in their stated tasks but we want a group to achieve optimum effectiveness. The conditions for an effective group are that the members are clear about the purpose and values. An established, agreed and written statement of values is one of the foundations of all effective activities.

In a new small group, pattern forming begins very quickly. If you start meetings late once or twice, you might expect that the impact is negligible. If you start late three or four times in a row, late starting becomes part of the culture. Humour at the expense of an individual is light-hearted and often acceptable, especially if there is a twinkle in the eyes. However, if the same person is the butt of two or three jokes, then an undermining culture has been established where it is acceptable to have whipping boys and girls. Patterns are formed after very few repeats of a type of behaviour. Above all, your first few decisions may not seem critical, and often the outcomes aren't, but how you come to them will be seen as pattern forming about how decision making will happen in the future. A few similar examples of any type of behaviour can quickly lead to a culture, easily established and hard to change.

In cell churches, where one of the principal aims of the group is that the group multiplies into two groups, there is an additional stage. During the "performing" stage, if it is done well, the group becomes too large to be a real community and splits into two. The danger is not only that groups grow too cosy, but also that great success causes parting to become especially painful and difficult. There needs to be a fresh emphasis on the "Welcoming" activity because there will be a significant number of new entrants just before the multiplication stage. The leader needs to focus on checking the values with the new people, before multiplication should be undertaken.

Behaviour reflects the values that we actually live, in reality, not the ones we state or espouse. Remember that the sum of the core values determines the corporate culture. To change the corporate culture of any organization requires certain key conditions, and is often reckoned to take at least two years. The basic requirements for changing the culture are that:

1. The existing culture is clearly understood.
2. The desired culture and the gap between the two cultures are clearly stated.
3. The senior leadership are individually and corporately committed to the change.
4. Either there are adequate change management skills "in-house" or additional external support and facilitation will prove necessary.
5. Activities that reflect the new culture are sustained and given the highest priority.

Often in church life all of these requirements are not met fully enough. Therefore experience seems to be suggesting that a fundamental change in church culture can take five years. This should not be a major surprise when you think how long we have spent reinforcing the prevalent culture in many of our churches. Imagine trying to shift the culture to the extent illustrated below:

Old culture characterized by:	New culture characterized by:
Ministry undertaken by one or a few people.	Every member ministering.
Inward looking.	Outward looking.
Pastoral care is maintenance.	People development.
Commitment to Sunday services only.	Motivated to a seven-day-week church mentality.
Small groups focus, if such groups exist, on teaching and prayer.	Small groups focus on discipleship and multiplication.
Seeing ourselves as miserable sinners.	Seeing ourselves as clothed in robes of righteousness.
Focusing on our problems.	Focusing on worshipping the God who is bigger than our problems.
Giving is based on the small change in our pockets.	Resources are needed; giving is a pleasure; tithing is a minimum.
Church is about Sunday meetings.	The midweek cell is the core unit of church life.
The church is thought of as a building.	The people are the church.

I am deliberately outlining two extreme possible churches, so that the contrast is stark and obvious. The amalgam of the changes illustrated above would take at least ten years. If the gap between the old and new cultures is less substantial, then the transition will be easier and shorter. Please note that I have primarily outlined changes in attitude, not an alteration in programme.

Purpose, values, vision and structures need a measure of compatibility and should be considered in this order. That's partly why we need to identify the purpose and values before we look at the vision. Appropriate structures are selected to give the best prospect of implementing the vision. Cell is a structure, often chosen for a vision based around numerical growth or discipleship. There must be a suitable set of values driving such a vision and structure. In other books on small groups, notably the Willow Creek guide, a set of values is quoted that is compatible for a church with a small group emphasis:

Affirmation
Availability
Prayer
Openness
Honesty
Safety
Confidentiality
Sensitivity
Accountability
Evangelism
Multiplication

I would not entirely agree with this list (any more than I would identify 100% with the examples that I gave earlier from the churches where I have recently worked!). First, for me, there are too many in this last list; and that always increases the possibility for tension between values. It will be very hard to satisfy them all. Safety and multiplication are not easy bedfellows, for example. Rapid multiplication increases risk. But above all, I do not see prayer, evangelism and multiplication as values; they are functions and expressions of priority. Doing these things is one thing, but how we set about them will make a statement about our values.

So the key points in summary are:

1. The core values deserve identifying and articulating.
2. The same values must be consistently held in all aspects and departments of church life.
3. Genuine ownership of, not just compliance with, the core values of the church is a key pre-requisite in recruiting potential small-group leaders.
4. Many of the conflicts within a small group are fundamentally about values.

Chapter **9**   *Vision*

I have written extensively about the subject of leadership in my first book (*Leadership Tool Kit*), but a brief summary is necessary at this juncture. The prime requirement of leadership is about the character of a person; we have said that values are caught and not taught, so the principal messages that leaders transmit are by doing more than saying. Nevertheless, we don't make all people of exemplary character into leaders.

I want to leave the subject of anointing alone for now, partly because, according to many people who focus on that sort of language, you either have it or not. There are no shops that sell anointing! That line of thinking easily links anointing to the gift of leadership, which is only mentioned once and even then within an extensive list of gifts (Romans 12:8). I am much more concerned with the many people who might be described as in the second tier of leadership, often involved in ministries like children's work, music and deaconing. Very frequently, leaders of small groups fall into this wider category.

The distinctiveness of leaders then, in addition to their character, is in function — what leaders actually do. They have two additional functions, quite different from the roles of other members; they give direction and they develop or disciple people. At any level of leadership, whatever the scale of responsibility, there has to be a sense of direction, a clear vision.

However, these functions have often been neglected and there are many reasons why this is so.

1. We have historically linked leader and pastor too closely. There are other leadership ministries apart from pastoral care.

2. We have emphasized servant leadership in the wrong way. Don't get me wrong; I believe in much of what has been said and written, but servant leadership is about the manner and motivation of leaders. It does not release them from the responsibilities of the two key functions.

3. We have cracked the old joke "You'll know who the leaders are; they have got followers" rather too often. The positive aspect of this quotation is that at least the leader is clearly going somewhere, but it may be read as an excuse that the ultimate calling of leaders is to generate followers. The final desire of the leader, apart from glorifying God, is that others should do greater things than they have done; holding people in followership will not encourage others to aspire to higher things; it only generates dependency.

4. We have relied on commitment, a sense of duty and obligation too much, rather than understanding how people are motivated. Without exploring the subject of motivation in detail, it is clear that different personalities are motivated both by different things and by different ways of doing things. Motivation is a very individualistic business. There is no cheap, effective version of leadership which gets away with treating everyone alike. A possible result of this mistaken thinking, focusing on commitment rather than motivation, is very serious. If attendance starts declining, the leader can tend to assume that folk are not sufficiently committed, rather than exploring the possibility that the group they lead is boring!

The bulk of this book is dedicated to development and discipleship, one of the core functions of leadership, but I want to address the subject of vision for the remainder of this chapter. I suppose that if I had only one scripture to call on for my introduction it would be Proverbs 29:18. There are rather different implications depending on which translation you consider, although scholars tell me that one or two of these translations are somewhat loose! Although the Authorised Version is the most familiar, they all seem to have a useful message for small-group leadership.

AV:	"Where there is no vision the people perish."
NIV and the RAV:	"Where there is no revelation the people cast off restraint."
RSV:	"Where there is no prophecy the people cast off restraint."
NEB:	"Where there is no one in authority the people break loose."
GNB:	"A nation without God's guidance is a nation without order."

Note that the passage does *not* say that without the *right* vision the people perish. Vision provides a way forward and if we acknowledge God in all our ways, he has promised to direct our paths (Proverbs 3:5–8). We will want to do our best, for obvious reasons, but the technology of vision-building is imperfect. Our ability to understand the future, and even our ability to hear God through our human filters, is tainted. Many is the time that I have been asked to consult with and facilitate a church leadership as it explores the issue of vision, and I've recognized that the reason for the lack of progress is that there is more than one vision in the room. Life would be much simpler if we all heard him say the same things. Nevertheless, I sometimes feel that God is saying, "Please aim for something. I can honour your efforts and fine tune the steering of a moving ship, but I cannot help your sense of direction if you stay paralysed at the quayside." The reason for the inertia may well be because of the fear that we might get it wrong.

When I started preparing materials on vision-building during the mid-1980s, I sensed that God gave me two very personal pictures. The first one was more of a recollection and dated back to my teaching days and the joys of supervising pupils waiting for the bus at the end of the school day. If school finished at 3.45 and the bus arrived at 3.50, the duty was not arduous, but if the bus did not arrive until 4.05, then the supervision was altogether more difficult. Pupils' idle hands will find something to do, statistically it's generally mischief, and often causes damage to each other! Churches have potentially similar dangers; hence the expression "The devil makes work for idle hands". People really do need a sense of direction to harness their energy constructively. My second picture was the tranquil image of a shepherd, and the flock grazing in lush pastures. The flock multiplied and in time the overworked pasture became sparse and barren. The message was that vision should bring life for a season, but not for ever. I know a fellowship that fell into this trap; the drive for starting a new church was largely the desire to be outside the formal structure of denominations and that understanding sustained them ten years ago as they were established. There hasn't been a clear vision since and they are quietly subsiding.

There are two principal dangers in the final vision statements that I find in churches and other organizations. First, the words "vision" and "plan" are wrongly used interchangeably; vision is about destination and planning is concerned with the route. By far the more common problem is that a statement of purpose is produced, believing it to be a vision. We need to look ahead to a point well beyond the present. Leadership thinking is about being able to make the macro leap from the present moment to that desired destination. In the setting of the full church I would consider time horizons of three to seven years. As a small-group leader, I recommend that you think about six to twelve months ahead. The vision could emerge from asking any combination of the following questions about the destination:

> What will we be thanking God for?
> What will we have become?
> What will we be celebrating?
> What will we be giving thanks for?
> What will we have caused?
> What will we be known for?
> What will we be known as?

Vision, whether it is for a church, a group or an individual, must meet the following criteria:

> **V**ital
> **I**nspiring
> **S**imple
> **I**nvolving
> **O**wned
> **N**ow

Vital
The vision must be at the centre of the life of the group, not related to just one or two individuals, nor to a narrow outcome. It must warrant the bulk of the energy of the whole group.

Inspiring
The vision must be worth the effort, enough to motivate members on cold, wet winter evenings when the day job has been extremely demanding. If in doubt, err on the side

of a vision that is too grand rather than too small. This is a good time for me to clarify an essential distinction; goals must be realistic and achievable, but not vision.

IF YOU CAN DO IT, IT'S NOT A VISION!

"A land flowing with milk and honey" is exciting but forty years trudging around in the desert on a limited diet is not motivating! It's the destination and the route contrast again.

Simple

The reason why so many vision statements are numerical is so that they are short and can be easily memorized. I am not advocating that all vision statements are numerical, many are qualitative or about reputation. While success criteria must enter the strategic planning process eventually, it is wrong to try and include too much information at the vision stage; the impact of the vision will be diluted too early. If the vision is simple, it can be communicated widely.

Involving

Ideally, every group member should see not just an opportunity for their involvement in the vision, but the vision's need for their personal commitment for there to be any prospect of success. If there is a sense that the vision can be attained with an extrapolation of the present trends, or by the efforts of only a few people, then there is no need for members to raise their game. We need to recognize that passionate people need a vision, but a vision also needs passionate people.

Owned

Attaining a vision is a team game. Vision has no inherent power until a wide constituency shares it. When the leader is talking about "my vision", we really haven't begun; when the group membership are talking about "our vision", then we have already made significant progress.

Now

At the beginning of the last decade, many vision statements were looking towards the year 2000 as their chosen time frame. As time went by without the vision influencing the activities, I had a feeling that 1999 would be a very busy year indeed if the visions were going to be accomplished! Too often, the result wasn't achieved because the nature of the vision was not easily translated into action. While vision is about looking forward to a desired destination, eventually, at the end of the planning process, vision must begin to impact what we are going to do next week. Vision always demands change and at the micro level, that must start somewhere. How do you eat an elephant? One mouthful at a time, starting with the first bite!

The acid test

A vision must contribute to our ability to prioritize. If a vision does not give a method of focusing on some areas of activity more than others, then I doubt if the outcome truly is a vision. Vision must never mean "more of the same in equal proportions". Consistently church leaders find that priorities are their biggest problem; there are so many things that we could do for God, which appear to have His hallmark on them. All meaningful visions will bring some clarity to this problem of what should we emphasize and do first.

In small groups, the difficulties that members tell me about are rather different from leaders' problems. Their single most frequent complaint stems from the time pressures on group leaders.

THE BIGGEST DANGER FOR A SMALL-GROUP LEADER, AND I MEAN THE SINGLE BIGGEST DANGER, IS TO LIMP ALONG FROM WEEK TO WEEK WITHOUT OFFERING SOME SENSE OF LONG-TERM DIRECTION.

All small-group leaders have fallen into this trap for an occasional evening at some time or other. "Goodness, it's Wednesday. What shall we do this evening?" Busk it, it will be all right on the night! The poorer the planning, the more likely we are to create a week-by-week programme rather than providing a direction supported by a cohesive and integrated package.

I used to teach maths and as an extra-curricula activity, sport. The plea from pupils was sometimes "Sir, what's the point of this?" It wasn't always easy to give a convincing answer, when the syllabus was omitting many mathematically based life skills, but did include geometry and algebra. Slightly similarly, sport could be prone to the same accusation, even if to a lesser degree. Unopposed exercises in rugby, and skills practices in small grids at football were only relevant if the pupils could imagine the application and consequent improvement in the competitive, full game situation. The same principles apply completely to small groups in churches. How does this week's programme or spiritual exercise equip me for the bigger picture? How does this week interface with last week? Where are we going in the next few weeks that will move us towards our vision? Too often, there are no convincing answers to these questions, and in church life, as opposed to maths, there should be! Members need to know and be able to see how the weekly content contributes towards the longer-term vision.

Obviously, it's important that the vision for the small group is consistent with, and subordinate to, the broader vision of the umbrella church. The small groups will appear very independent if there is no bigger picture for them to serve.

I want to close this chapter with a reminder of how purpose, values and vision fit together. The importance of the top box goes without saying, but vision is generally subordinate to purpose and values. A vision will usually remain valid for a much shorter period. I have never known any organization, church or group produce a vision which has served them well and made a difference, without first visiting their purpose and values. (I have marked all the arrows as two-way, since vision can challenge our existing values and even our understanding of God's word.)

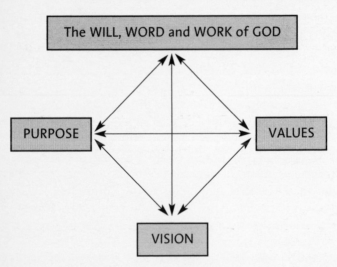

Many of the materials in this chapter have been written about previously and more comprehensively by my colleague and friend, David Cormack, in *Change Directions: New ways forward for your life, church and business* (Monarch, 1995). Unfortunately, the book is out of print at the moment, but if you can find a copy, please read it. Technically, it is the best book written on this subject, based on very wide experience in this field. I gladly acknowledge his permission to quote so extensively, but even more, thank him for coaching me in this area during the eighties. The book can be obtained on a CD direct from the author.

Part 3 The Skills of Small-group Leadership

Chapter 10 Transitioning of Structures

The management of change is concerned with the methodology of implementing the vision. If vision is about where we are going, then the management of change is about how we will get there. For the purposes of this book, we are concerned with change in one direction only. I know of no examples of cell churches that have transitioned to any other format. It can only be a matter of time, however, before a cell church "mutates" into another format; no structure is for ever.

The management of change has several key components:

1. Clarify the vision
Despite some literature advocating one pure model of cell church, in practice the outcomes have proved rather different in various churches. Give a sharp, graphic picture of your destination. All that we said about vision for a small group can be conceptually applied to the bigger picture of the whole church and could usefully be reread if your church is about to change structural shape.

2. Be realistic about the present situation
Old Testament prophets were very realistic and almost brutal about describing the present scenario. Nowadays gags like "Well, if I were you, I wouldn't start from here!" are decidedly unhelpful!

3. Planning

Planning can simply be defined as the steps that need to be taken to get us from where we are to where we want to be. It is often a fairly easy process if we have been accurate in describing the starting point and the finishing line, and quite impossible without those two limits! I frequently used to visit Newcastle, and a secretary faithfully sent me a street map for each trip. The venue was vividly highlighted in fluorescent colour, but to this day, I don't know where my route should have first appeared on the map. My navigation was solely by the road signs and the map brought little advantage. Church life can be very similar; a realistic appraisal of the present (the starting point) is just as important to planning as the vision's contribution.

4. The human factors

Often the greatest failure in change management is the failure to gain the real commitment of the majority of the people. The human ownership produces the change in the corporate culture and encompasses attitudes as well as behaviour. A major structural change can be implemented at the stroke of a pen, but these more emotional issues are bound to take much longer to resolve. Different churches have quoted figures from three to five years for the full adoption of cells.

All the principles of GODLY planning are in the following reading. May I encourage you to read this long passage with all the detail; please savour the full picture. I still find a real reluctance in churches to plan; I'm not sure whether planning is seen as "unspiritual" or whether life is seen as too unpredictable to make planning worth while. It causes me real concern when I find leaders who want the congregation to leave their brains at the door when they enter church; I suspect that they may also want them to leave their spiritual dimension at the door when they go to work!

This passage comprehensively refutes this pseudo-spiritual approach.

1 Chronicles 28:1–19

(1) David summoned all the officials of Israel to assemble at Jerusalem: the officers over the tribes, the commanders of the divisions in the service of the king, the commanders of thousands and commanders of hundreds, the officials in charge of all the property and livestock belonging to the king and his sons, together with the palace officials, the mighty men and all the brave warriors.

(2) King David rose to his feet and said: "Listen to me, my brothers and my people. I had it in my heart to build a house as a place of rest for the ark of the covenant of the Lord, for the footstool of our God, and I made plans to build it. (3) But God said to me 'You are not to build a house for my Name, because you are a warrior and have shed blood.'

(4) "Yet the Lord, the God of Israel, chose me from my whole family to be king over Israel for ever. He chose Judah as leader, and from the house of Judah he chose my family, and from my father's sons he was pleased to make me king over all Israel. (5) Of all my sons — and the Lord has given me many — he has chosen my son Solomon to sit on the throne of the kingdom of the Lord over Israel. (6) He said to me, 'Solomon your son is the one who will build my house and my courts, for I have chosen him to be my son, and I will be his father. (7) I will establish his kingdom for ever if he is unswerving in carrying out my commands and laws, as is being done at this time.'

(8) "So now I charge you in the sight of all Israel and of the assembly of the Lord, and in the hearing of our God: Be careful to follow all the commands of the Lord your God, that you may possess this good land and pass it on as an inheritance to your descendants for ever.

(9) "And you, my son Solomon, acknowledge the God of your father, and serve him with wholehearted devotion and with a willing mind, for the Lord searches every heart and understands every motive behind the thoughts. If you seek

him, he will be found by you; but if you forsake him, he will reject you for ever. (10) Consider now, for the Lord has chosen you to build a temple as a sanctuary. Be strong and do the work."

(11) Then David gave his son Solomon the plans for the portico of the temple, its buildings, its storerooms, its upper parts, its inner rooms and the place of atonement. (12) He gave him the plans of all that the Spirit had put in his mind for the courts of the temple of the Lord and all the surrounding rooms, for the treasuries of the temple of God and for the treasuries for the dedicated things. (13) He gave him instructions for the divisions of the priests and Levites, and for all the work of serving in the temple of the Lord, as well as for all the articles to be used in its service. (14) He designated the weight of gold for all the gold articles to be used in various kinds of service, and the weight of silver for all the silver articles to be used in various kinds of service: (15) the weight of gold for the gold lampstands and their lamps, with the weight for each lampstand and its lamps; and the weight of silver for each silver lampstand and its lamps, according to the use of each lampstand; (16) the weight of gold for each table for consecrated bread; the weight of silver for the silver tables; (17) the weight of pure gold for the forks, sprinkling bowls and pitchers; the weight of gold for each gold dish; and the weight of silver for each silver dish; (18) the weight of refined gold for the altar of incense. He also gave him the plan for the chariot, that is, the cherubim of gold that spread their wings and shelter the ark of the covenant of the Lord

(19) "All this," David said, "I have in writing from the hand of the Lord upon me, and he gave me understanding in all the details of the plan."

The management of change is a conceptually difficult subject to sub-divide. All the key ingredients are illustrated in this passage.

1. Discontent

Any major change starts with a good reason; don't scratch if you are not itching! "Contentment" has a pleasant resonance but it is very close to complacency and apathy in terms of our capacity to change. In this case in the passage, and in many other situations, repentance is the driving force behind discontentment (1 Chronicles 21:8,17). Leaders should state very clearly the perceived shortfall which they hope that a major initiative will address. Please note that members move forward on the basis of their discontent, not on the leaders' discontent with them! Sometimes the leaders have to highlight the discontent as the starting point of the process. There are many other passages that stress this discontent factor, including Habakkuk 1:1–4 and virtually the whole of Haggai 1. Arousing and focusing on discontent is like playing with fire, but it's necessary if we want to warm up! The most common reasons for adopting cell-church strategies are usually the lack of numerical growth and effective evangelism, or sometimes the lack of real discipleship.

2. The vision

The vision is right at the start of this biblical communication in verse 2. "I had it in my heart to build a house as a place of rest for the Ark of the Covenant of the Lord, for the footstool of our God and I made plans to build it." All the remaining text is subordinate to that single vision statement. Neither is this passage unique; the creation account would offer much the same principle, the vision statement (Genesis 1:1), and then the detail.

3. Planning is an activity of the heart

We don't just want compliance; we want people to be passionate about the prospects of improvement. The heart is where the emotion is seated. Elsewhere in the Psalms, we read about the desires of our heart (eg Psalm 20:4; 37:4). We need to acknowledge them at a personal level and take account of them as we plan at a corporate level. In both chapters 28 and 29 of 1 Chronicles, verse 9, we find the word "wholehearted", not for example, whole spirited.

When we hope that people will share in great adventures with us, we need to appeal and influence at the emotional, not just the rational level. It takes a wholehearted commitment to see through a long process of change, not only an academic and intellectual assent.

4. Planning is also at the spiritual level

In verse 12 we read that it was the Spirit that had communicated with him. I cannot over stress the spiritual dimension of the planning process; we need to know the Holy Spirit's guidance and that our interpretation lines up with his revealed word.

5. Planning is an activity of the mind

The passage does not say that the Spirit communicates with our spirit. The deposit was into his mind. Later on, in verse 19, we are told that he had understanding in all the details of the plan, also presumably, in the mind. Long-term strategic thinking is hard work; most people are more comfortable with shorter time frames and more immediate results.

6. Major change involves quality communication

The whole passage is a substantial keynote speech delivered with passion. The quality of your communications will have a substantial bearing on how quickly and smoothly the transition progresses.

7. The commitment of the wider leadership is critical to the success of a major change

The assembled gathering is listed in chapter 28, verse 1 and chapter 29, verse 6. They are all leaders, with a wide range and variety of responsibilities. Make sure that before you set forth on any major transition, the wider leadership are with you in heart, mind and spirit. The alternative is reliance on blind obedience and the collective responsibility of joint leadership (toeing the party line under a three-line whip). Admittedly during the change process, you might lose a few people on the way, but make sure that the leadership are fully with you at the outset. Quite a proportion of the total time in the process is spent gaining this commitment; it's an investment not a waste of time. These are the people who later must take other people with you, for you. As we shall see soon, it is difficult to personally influence everybody effectively; the other leaders act as your associate change agents.

You cannot have too many prospective leaders/interns. It has often been said that the cell-church structure has a leadership focus not a small-group emphasis. While I think that this conclusion is debatable, the experience of many churches who have made the transition is that the support of the wider leadership is vital. Here is a quote from Alan Meyer, the senior pastor at St Paul's Elim Church in Carlisle, which has been a pioneer cell church within the Elim movement. I gladly acknowledge a debt of gratitude for all that they have taught me.

> Prior to transition, our second tier was a very limited group of deacons and departmental leaders. As we have developed our community groups (their title for cells) we have increased our total leadership by 250%! The quality and style of those leaders has also changed and in effect our new leadership structure comprises elders, group leaders and deacons. The role of the deacons has altered from having a degree of leadership to a management role, and the spiritual leadership is now the responsibility of the cell leaders and their zone supervisors, under the overall direction of the elders. The new second tier of leadership is enthusiastic, based upon a serving attitude and very committed in terms of time and energy. Many leaders have emerged, some of whom would never have been recognized or developed under our previous structure, and the overwhelming feeling is that this has been a very positive step for the church.

The thrust of Alan's comments would be echoed by other cell-church leaders. Invest deeply in the leaders that you have and expect others to emerge.

We now need to spend a little time considering how to take the bulk of the individual members with us. Perhaps the most important message revolves around the fact that some people adopt new ideas faster than others. Therefore it must be possible for more questioning and sceptical people to "catch the second train" without being branded as "lacking in faith", and without losing credibility. Experience has taught these cautious people that sometimes it is worth waiting at the junction because those people who caught the first train are often back there soon, having found that the latest new fad was a cul-de-sac rather than the main line!

Dr Eddie Gibbs and Dr David Cormack have both written about four broad clusters of people who form a continuum about their attitude towards change: radicals, progressives, conservatives and traditionalists.

Radicals
They shout "Yes" first and then ask where we are going later. All change is good, by definition. Anything must be better than repetition.

Progressives
Change is the norm. We respect the radicals. We sometimes make mistakes but the world is moving on and so do we, gladly.

Conservatives
Change is grudgingly acknowledged as necessary, but proceed with caution, after asking lots of questions. Assume that most proposed changes are not good.

Traditionalists
The answer is "No" so you need not bother with the details. All change is bad and needs to be resisted or these radicals will have us following every possible latest whim and flavour of the month. It was never better than in the "good old days".

Obviously, if we only wanted to take the radicals with us, we could set forth immediately, and if we waited for the last die-hard traditionalist, we would never go forward. So the question is, how many, and which people, form the critical population to move the whole body forward?

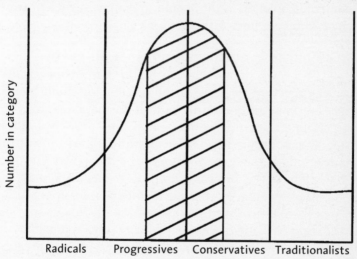

The informal opinion makers
In the middle of this continuum, there will be more progressives and conservatives than at the edges, where you find the radicals and traditionalists. The noise is made at the edges, with the radicals shouting "Yes" and the traditionalists screaming "No". Somewhere in the middle you have the minority of about 10% of your membership who are vital if you are going to move forward with cohesion.

They are progressive/conservatives or conservative/progressives. They are not vociferous; their support is by doing rather than backslapping. But they do influence other people; if people from this group say "It is OK" then it really is an acceptable change. They encourage the radicals to exercise a little patience and caution and gently encourage the traditionalists to take measured steps forward. They hear and understand the concerns at the edges of the spectrum. They influence out of who they are, not the position that they hold. You need to write down the names of these people; members of the leadership team need to spend time with them on a one-to-one basis. If you have persuaded this group of people, the right people, and allow sufficient time, they will take others with you, for you.

Influencing is a process, not just an event

It can be a stark shaft of realization for a minister or elder to recognize that the bulk of the influencing might not be done by them and certainly not via formal "meetings" or preaching. The critical conversations are often over coffee after church, around the last car in the car park, or waiting for the kids outside the primary-school gates at 3.15 pm. This is where the informal opinion makers operate. The phalanx of opinion is eventually won one person at a time, as much as by inspirational presentations. Just as we read in 1 Chronicles, major change today requires conviction in the heart, mind and spiritual dimensions; change must be a "whole person" activity. All too frequently, attempts to influence are at the rational level and don't take account of the possible emotional barriers to change, like personal history, the fear of the unknown, etc.

ONCE YOU ANNOUNCE THE VISION, MOST OF YOUR METHODS OF GAINING COMMITMENT HAVE GONE.

Numbers 13:1 – 14:10

This passage about Moses and the role of change agents has some additional key messages and easy parallels for us today. I think that we can learn from his mistakes as well as some of his good management of change.

V. 1. God was giving the land to the Israelites; Moses had that promise to rely on throughout the process. He had heard God speak to him, right at the beginning of the process.

V. 2. The group he sent as representatives were all leaders. We have affirmed how important the wider leadership team is during our transitions. God asked them to spy out the land, although he had given it to them. Similarly, we need to understand our "destination", even if he has spoken.

Vv. 17-20. Moses gave them detailed instructions, but did not mention that God had given them the land. If you are sure that you have God's word on the issue, there might be a case for saying so.

V. 26. Moses lost control of the process by allowing the spies' report to go to the whole community, rather than just to the leaders.

Vv. 28-33. If a vote had been taken, the result would have been 2 in favour of moving into the land and 10 against the motion. Democracy is not the best form of decision-making (hindsight is!).

Chapter 14:1-10 shows us the many bad fruits of the resulting conflict caused by poor change management:

A. The word "all" appears frequently. There was a polarization of the responses.

B. There was a loss of reality, forgetting what Egypt had really been like and now wanting to return there.
C. There were doubts about God's favour towards them (v.8).
D. When in doubt, stone the leaders!

Fortunately, God shows up in the nick of time! (v.10).

I have deliberately kept the materials of this chapter at a general level, hoping that you can make the bridges and links so that insights are applicable to both the whole church and the small group. Change is seldom easy and often stressful. There is always a cost. However, we sometimes need to offer the encouragement, that the price of NOT changing can be even higher.

Summary
1. The organizational elements of change include understanding of the destination and the present situation.
2. The human problem concerns gaining commitment, at a heart, mind and spiritual level.
3. Communication is therefore critical.

Chapter *11*

Leading Discussions and Asking Questions

In this chapter, I want us to consider some of the basic principles and skills of small group dynamics. The more conscious we are of these features, the more likely that we will continue to improve in our leadership of an evening meeting.

Size of the group

Many leaders of small groups have experienced the problems that can occur when the group is either too large or too small. Roughly the minimum number in a group needs to be five people and the maximum should not be above twelve. If the group is too small, it is often difficult to generate a lively discussion (especially if some people are very reserved) and obviously it is hard to give everybody an opportunity to contribute if the group is too large (especially if some members are particularly vocal). But this broad analysis might mask a few other important factors. We need to take into consideration not just the number of people nominally attached to the group, but the actual average attendance. For example, if the church is subdivided into clusters of ten for the purposes of small groups, and the average attendance is 60% across the whole church, many groups will be in danger of being too small on some evenings. If there are different people attending from one week to the next, discussions will be especially slow to gather momentum.

The range of people attending the group

In some ways it is much easier to lead a fairly homogeneous group, than a group with a wide range of maturity, experiences and expectations. Depending on the purpose of the group, there might be visitors and people who are not Christians, let alone a full spectrum of backgrounds from within the church membership. The variety of contributions from a diverse group can be constructive and beneficial to every member of the group, but the group is generally more difficult to lead. Good group leaders will be particularly sensitive about the use of language and vocabulary; the wrong use of jargon and in-house humour can be very isolating for a new group member.

Purpose and process

Leaders must be absolutely clear in their own mind what they want from the discussion component of the evening and the shorter the time allocation for the discussion element, the more important it is to be clear about the purpose. Questions like these should form an integral part of the preparation:

What do you want to achieve by the discussion?
How will you know when you have got there?
How flexible are you prepared to be over process issues and time allocation?
How important is it that everybody contributes this week?

The good leader always has *purpose* and *process* at the front of their mind. It is good to share the purpose with the members at the beginning of the discussion; they can only help you reach your intended destination if they know where you want to go!

Frequently, the reason for the inclusion of a discussion is that it is a more effective way of learning than a monologue. The possible danger here is that the leader decides the desired conclusions before the discussion starts and then subtly steers the contributions towards that destination. The solution to this danger lies in revisiting the whole purpose of the discussion. It is far better if our purposes include outcomes like:

> To enable members to come to their own conclusions about....
> For members to be aware of the range of opinions about....
> To challenge widely held paradigms about....

Leaders should frequently check that they really have emotionally let go of the conclusions; there will usually be more than one right answer.

Handling the contributions

Ultimately we want the discussion to flow across the room from member to member without every contribution being directed through the leader. If the leader is making alternate contributions, probably they have not really relinquished control and the discussion will be stifled. A discussion with more varied dynamics is much livelier and the contributions are likely to be a better reflection of the member's true thoughts and feelings. Also, the learning caused by the discussion is probably deeper within each member. It is not always easy for the leader to generate a discussion without remaining the fulcrum; acquiring this skill is sometimes a major breakthrough for an intern.

The whole group can and should take the responsibility for improving the quality of the discussion. This would be proper evidence of a group that believes in "one anothering"! Any member can deter the verbose contributor and anyone can encourage the reticent person. It does not have to be the "formal" leader who says things like:

> "Let's hear from some of the others at this point."
> "What do you think about that, Jenny?"
> "Hold on for a minute, Ken. Perhaps others would like the opportunity to chip in here."
> "What does anybody else feel/think about that?"

This style of group leadership, applicable especially to discussions, is sometimes called the "open chair". Often the best discussions occur within a mature group, clearly understanding the purpose of the discussion and sharing the responsibility to generate lively dynamics in this way. There are occasions when the group leader may have to draw the discussion back on course. So there are two ends of the spectrum of discussion styles, each with attendant dangers: the "free for all" and the leader-dominated discussion.

Don't be too concerned about silence. Be prepared to wait for others to step in. Some years ago the Radio 1 cult become popular; many people seemed almost afraid of their own company without additional noise. Children now say that they do homework better while listening to music. I believe that this distaste of silence has cost us dearly in the failure to really enjoy biblical meditation and that the same thinking can hamper a small-group discussion. If you are fairly sure that you have asked the right question, don't feel that you have to rush in with the answer or an alternative way to phrase the question.

Group discussions should be an opportunity to learn. We need to model this as group leaders, by being prepared to shift our own views and opinions during the course of a discussion. Remember too, that other people may be formulating their opinions as they speak! Mouth is sometimes engaged before mind as we think things through. Initial comments and reactions are not always the same as final conclusions.

In closing this section on discussions, I want to make some very brief points:

1. Give feedback, especially by thanking people for their contributions.
2. Expect everybody to contribute, but not in equal measure.
3. Differentiate between facts and opinions and encourage others to do likewise.
4. Be sensitive and particularly grateful for personal disclosures that attempt to deepen the level of sharing.

Discussions in cells

The contrast between homegroups and cells is very evident when it comes to the discussion element of the evening meeting. Many traditional homegroups that are primarily focused on Bible study may well spend the bulk of the evening in discussion mode. Assuming that a cell is following the four "W"s format, the discussion component will be much shorter. At first sight the cell-group leader is facing a more difficult task in trying to generate a meaningful discussion in a much shorter time, and still wanting everybody to have an opportunity to contribute. I suspect, however, that there are some favourable factors to compensate for the lack of time. First, the four "W"s model is widely talked about in cell churches; people understand the time pressures and are clear about the purposes of the small-group meeting. Secondly, some cells are relatively small by design, to leave room for new members; the by-product is that everyone can still contribute during a shorter discussion. Thirdly, because the small group is seen as so critical to church life, the percentage attendance rate may be generally much higher than in other structures. This is a positive feature, because the discussion dynamics are then more predictable, which is more comfortable for the individual members.

At the point when the cell multiplies, the dynamics will change dramatically. For many leaders, particularly in those churches that have transitioned to cell from another church structure, it may be a real test of attitude. It is easy to have a residual sense of the larger the group, the more important I feel as a pastor. I meet many small group leaders still wanting to lead larger groups. Even shepherds want to be wanted by the sheep! The worship might sound more convincing as well! Less questionably, there can be a very natural and understandable grieving in seeing friends moving on, even if it is to form a new group.

Questions

The realization that questions can be far more effective than statements has revolutionized my ministry in the last few years. Once the penny had dropped, I set about consciously improving my skills in the area of questioning. There were probably two phases of improvement, albeit with very blurred boundaries:

> Asking the right questions in the wrong way, a little too like an interrogation,
> Asking the right questions in a more natural and relaxed way.

If you sense that you are in the first phase, don't be discouraged. People will continue to accept your questions, as long as the general relationship has a solid foundation. In a similar way, don't be afraid of sometimes asking a direct question to a quiet group member.

Questions can be used negatively, for example to maintain verbal ascendancy, to put people down or to expose vulnerability. Having checked our motives against these dangers, I obviously don't want to dwell on that type of questioning. We can also ask questions for a wide variety of positive reasons:

> To gain more information.
> To start a discussion.
> To seek clarification.
> To generate learning.
> To bring about change.

The opening question in launching a discussion in a small group is a key moment in the evening. At best it can stimulate a good flow of debate very quickly or, at worst, a bad question can cost the group ten minutes. The first question must address the right subject, have a wide range of "correct" answers, and contain interest and sufficient provocation. The leadership of the discussion section of the evening is often delegated; this section does not have to be led by the group leader. The opportunity is there in any church structure, including cells, but in no way restricted to cells. If the person leading the discussion element has no other responsibility during the evening, they may well take more care in formulating the initial trigger question.

A reflective statement can be just as effective as a question, without seeming quite so direct and potentially threatening. Comments like:

> "I can see how exposed you must have felt."
> "That must have been very challenging."
> "On top of everything else, that was a difficult time for the family."
> "Then you were emotionally very concerned about that decision."

All of these statements contain a measure of invitation, drawing the listener into the conversation, and offering them the chance to amplify their previous comments or correct your summary. Even if your reflective statement is a tentative conclusion, the tone of voice can still make the invitation clear.

In earlier chapters I have said that the small group should be a genuine community within the church. The depth of sharing during the discussion phase of the evening, illustrating trust levels, is a good indicator of the quality of community life. A timely and appropriate personal disclosure can change both the evening meeting and the resultant learning. Questions involving "Why?" and "How?" generally have the highest potential for yielding quality responses. Often the second question, the probe, following up a first bland answer, can encourage people to make the discussion more significant. The second answer is sometimes less important than the messages given by your second question; you are asking for a depth of sharing and will not be satisfied with superficial discussion. Useful probes include:

"How do you mean?"
"How can you be sure?"
"What would be the implications of that?"
"What would be the counter arguments?"
"Could there be any other solutions?"
"Would you like to expand on that last point?"

Summary
1. Think through the time limitations and the purpose of the discussion in your preparation.
2. The question launching the discussion is critical to the quality of the discussion.
3. Reflective statements and probes are acceptable ways of taking the discussion deeper.

Chapter **12**   *Listening*

James 1:19 says, "My dear brothers, take note of this: every-one should be quick to listen, slow to speak and slow to become angry."

The politically correct phrase "valuing people" seems to have drifted into use in the church. The reasons are sound and the concept is good. Yet too often, in both the "church" and the "world", the phrase is used without much substance; we are not clear about the practical behaviour that should be the flesh on the bones of the concept. I want to suggest that listening to people, in a constructive, active way, must be a fundamental expression of how we value them. It is therefore a core skill for the small-group leader, and one that we should be continually developing in others and ourselves. To go the "second mile" in listening will show an interest in the person because we have gone beyond the basic content of the message. A decade ago, the hints in books like this one focused on how we can draw out the quiet person, and sometimes there is still this need within small groups. However, I am increasingly finding, especially within the rush of attempting all four "W"s every week, that the quality of listening is declining; it's virtually the opposite problem nowadays.

It is generally reckoned that communication is made up of:

Words	7%
Speech	38% (which includes tone, volume, pace and pauses)
Non-verbal	55%

The implications of these figures are very powerful. You might be surprised that the selection of the words contributes such a very low percentage to our communication. Nevertheless, we need to be particularly careful in our choice of vocabulary, partly for the sake of visitors and new members. The odd long theological word can prove an insurmountable barrier to understanding and make a significant negative impact on an otherwise pleasant evening. If you have ever watched any general knowledge quizzes on television, you may have noticed how little biblical knowledge most people have today. There is no reason to suppose that the unchurched person who has just started attending the small group is substantially different.

It is surprising, given the incompleteness of written communication, that so many difficult situations are dealt with by letter. I appreciate that many people find conflict-type meetings highly stressful and prefer to put their thoughts on paper in a measured way. I would advocate the greater benefits of meeting face to face and summarizing the outcome in writing. Certainly there is the danger that different things are remembered as significant after such a meeting, so written agreement of the events and subsequent action plans are very constructive, but not to the exclusion of the added dimensions of fuller communication. E-mail is being used increasingly as a method of pastoral contact between meetings, especially used by people in full-time employment. I suspect that research might show that the receivers barely consider this type of care to be meaningful. Use the written mode as an additional tool, not as a substitute, in virtually every level of communication.

The speech component of communication includes

variations (hopefully!) of volume, pitch, pace and the use of pauses. Speech gives meaning to the words. The same words can mean quite different things when spoken in a different style. A sentence that could be quite hurtful and cutting can be robbed of all offence by the manner of delivery. Interesting voices use varying combinations of the features of speech to sustain our listening. Pace has a particularly powerful impact. The human ear, with much practice, can absorb words at the rate of 500 per minute; this has been researched using sophisticated tape recorders. The average adult rate of speaking is 120 words per minute. Admittedly, there is nothing worse than people speaking so quickly that the words are garbled, but another great danger, especially when we are tired, is that listeners become bored, waiting for the right word to be selected and for sentences to be finished. Easy listening can usually be achieved by speaking relatively quickly combined with the judicious use of pauses. Some people are blessed by a timbre to their voice that makes them easier to focus on for longer periods of time. We all have a choice, obviously, as to how much we work on these issues. I'm not advocating trying to change so radically that we hardly recognize ourselves, but we have responsibilities for our contribution in communication.

Another corollary of these percentages quoted above is that we are using only 45% of our potential communication when we are talking over the telephone. When there are no anticipated difficulties, the phone is a great method of keeping in touch. (I'll begin to sound like an advertisement soon!) Make sure that humour is used carefully during telephone conversations. Phrases that have the potential to be misinterpreted are dangerous. If the twinkle in your eye would be the saving grace in a face-to-face chat, then the words will be ambiguous on the telephone.

This leaves us with the most significant component of communication, the non-verbal aspects (55%). There are two further principal sub-divisions which can be explored. Some elements of non-verbal communication are relatively "fixed" throughout a conversation or small-group evening, things like hairstyle, make-up, manner of dress and design of spectacles. The remainder are about body language. Body language, therefore, is a sub-set of non-verbal communication but not the whole story.

These statistics underline the importance of non-verbal communication, and of body language in particular, as the most significant components within all communication. Please be assured that I am not encouraging any attempt to lie with body language, for two good reasons: first, it would be sinful, and secondly, I don't believe that it could be sustained! The important thing to recognize is that the ingredients of communication operate together, not in isolation. We are understood, and deemed credible and trustworthy when our verbal and non-verbal communications are congruent. I'm suggesting that your gut reaction to a speaker is therefore probably accurate because, usually subconsciously, we are evaluating not only the words that people use, but also the accompanying body language. Years ago, one of the television companies did some research about the credibility of newsreaders and found that impressions of their trustworthiness varied very widely. It's the combination of the verbal and non-verbal elements of communication that determine acceptance. You can illustrate the importance of the non-verbal elements very easily. Turn the volume down to mute on the television and you will still understand the gist of what is being communicated.

There are quite a few books available on body language and I recommend a little caution in what you choose to take from them. Too often, inferences are based on one individual snapshot of a non-verbal communication; that can be just as misleading and ambiguous as a single spoken word taken in isolation. But trust your overall impressions of any communication because that will be based on thousands of non-verbal snapshots during a short time span.

The implication of the importance of the non-verbal communication is that we virtually need to redefine listening. We need to use not only our ears but also our eyes in terms of really understanding the contributions during a small-group meeting. The leader's concentration level needs to be very high if the finger is going to be truly on the pulse.

Two other skills deserve mentioning as part and parcel of listening and the first one is called attending. Attending can be defined as showing that you are listening. Some of the contributory feedback gestures will be non-verbal, like nodding your head; other possibilities could be verbal like "I see", "Good", "OK", or "Fine". During seminars on the subject of communication skills, I sometimes include one-minute exercises to illustrate the importance of this type of feedback. Working in pairs, or with a third person observing, I ask the "transmitter" to talk for one minute on an interesting but prescribed subject. The "receiver" is asked to listen carefully and later will be required to repeat back to the transmitter the content of the message. The only unusual requirement of the exercise is that the "receiver" must give no encouragement, feedback or affirmation to the "transmitter". (One delegate started taking his shoes and socks off as he was listening very carefully!) It is highly disconcerting to speak into this sort of vacuum. I am using this example to illustrate that we need to select an appropriate level of attending; obviously too much can be obtrusive and unhelpful.

Eye contact is a very important part of attending. It is much easier to listen when we are giving a "transmitter" the right amount of eye contact. The "appropriate level" is not always easy to define, since none is discourteous and too much is confrontational. In settings where various cultures are represented, the balance can be particularly tricky, and there is always the danger of misinterpretation between sexes.

As a small-group leader, it is important not just that we listen, but that we show that we are listening. I am convinced that some members' contributions are too long because they do not perceive that they have been heard. Sometimes they have been heard but their contribution has not been accepted. Whatever the reason, if there has been insufficient feedback, then often they will repeat the same message in different words until there is a clear response.

A second skill associated with listening is that of rephrasing and reflecting. Having listened to a contribution you summarize it and bounce it back in this sort of format:

> "If I'm understanding you correctly, what you are saying is..."
>
> "If I'm hearing you right, then..."

This is excellent feedback in any situation, but is particularly handy after a long contribution or an emotional one. It provides a summary for other members who might have lost the thread of the contribution and gives the immediate opportunity for the speaker to correct us if we have attributed the wrong emphasis. There is clearly a risk that in affirming your understanding, they will repeat the whole saga, but more typically, you are exposing that the contribution could have been abbreviated.

Listening is a key activity for members and leaders of small groups, whether the structure is based on cells, Bible studies or any other reason for meeting. My prime reason for this assertion was outlined at the beginning of the chapter: listening is one of the principal methods of truly valuing people. In cells particularly, the icebreaker (welcome activity) is a time when the leader must listen (with ears and eyes!) carefully. The information gleaned at this stage may well impact the priorities for the whole evening.

How are the members today? Are there any general concerns?

Questionnaire

This exercise is designed to audit some of our attitudes and behaviours associated with listening. Your immediate responses are probably the most useful and accurate. Please complete each of the following sentences:

1. I regularly give positive feedback to a speaker by

2. I can sustain my concentration when I am listening to somebody who

3. The most memorable sermons/talks/seminars that I have heard are characterized by

4. I find the following traits in speakers rather off-putting

5. Topics which I find quite disconcerting include

6. When I am bored with listening, I often find myself

7. If there is little opportunity for me to make a contribution, I tend to

8. The basic attitudes that underpin my worst listening are

9. When I critically examine myself as a listener, I conclude that

10. I could best improve my listening by

Years ago, I found this reading framed at a friend's home. (To my knowledge, it's anonymous.) I use it in closing to illustrate the power and benefits of listening:

Listening

When I ask you to listen to me and you start giving me advice, you have not done what I asked.

When I ask you to listen to me and you begin to tell me why I shouldn't feel that, you are trampling on my feelings.

When I ask you to listen to me and you feel you have to do something to solve my problem, you have failed me, strange as that may seem.

Listen!

All I asked was that you listen, not talk or do; just hear me.

Advice is cheap.

And I can do for myself: I'm not helpless. Maybe discouraged and faltering, but not helpless.

When you do something for me *that I can and need to do for myself,* you contribute to fear and weakness.

But, when you accept as a simple fact that I do feel what I feel, no matter how irrational, then I can quit trying to convince you and get about the business of understanding what's behind this irrational feeling. And when that's clear, the answers are obvious and I don't need advice.

Irrational feelings make sense when you know what's behind them.

So, please listen and just hear me.

And if you want to talk, wait a minute for your turn; and I'll listen to you.

Chapter 13 Handling Tricky Situations

Many of the books about how to lead small groups offer rather trite solutions to the problems that we face during the meetings, especially the relational issues. It's just not possible in a few lines of text to convey every aspect of a scenario or to club together many different situations under a ballpark heading. As we have already outlined, much of your information will have been gleaned non-verbally and therefore cannot be conveyed to a reader. Many other factors will come into play as you think through your possible solutions, including your preferred leadership style, any history of similar situations within the group, the depth of the problem, the timing and your skill level. We can all too easily fall into the trap of stereotyping problems into a few clusters and prescribe one universal solution for each cluster of difficulties. Those solutions would be unrealistic generalizations.

The bulk of the conflict that we experience is negative and destructive. We need to distinguish within the small-group meeting between:

the small proportion that is likely to produce good fruit in our lives,

the major component which causes harm and over which we have considerable control,

and the minority of occurrences which we seem unable to predict or manage.

Apart from the discernment needed to judge between the rare positive and frequent negative potential, small-group leaders must be continually honing their skills in the area of conflict resolution. We need to understand that there will always be a degree of tension between the different hopes and expectations of the following stakeholders:

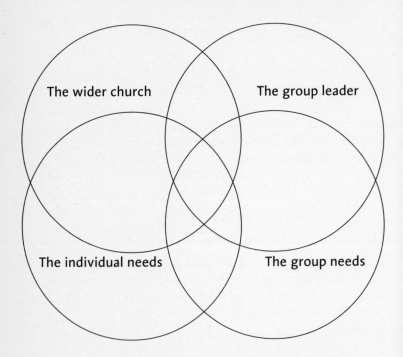

The wider church

The group leader

The individual needs

The group needs

When we recognize that the balance between these demands is less than ideal, there is the additional danger of over-compensating. Group behaviour often oscillates around the ideal position and the leader must ensure that the magnitude of the swings is within acceptable limits.

From day to day we are faced with many types of problem and there is seldom only one right solution; small-group life is similar. Here are six types of problem with illustrations:

Type of problem	Example in every day life
1. The one right answer	Solution to a crossword clue, the correct bar code, a telephone number, a flight time. Answers on *Who wants to be a millionaire?*
2. The surprise	A mistake that produces a new idea. "POST ITs" were invented by accident.
3. The unpredictable	A problem which can only be solved by trial and error. Customer reaction to new products, the different possible medical diagnoses to a set of symptoms.
4. The iceberg	A problem which looks small on the surface. That small spot of rust on the side of the car! A few comments on the surface of a deeper relationship problem.
5. The jelly	A problem which is very hard to pin down. What foods are good for you?
6. The combination	The unpredictable, jelly iceberg! Most problems that occur in small groups!

(The concept of these types was first published in David Cormack's course notes *Creative Problem Solving*, 1995.)

Probably the most frequent types of problem that we face in small-group leadership are either the "jelly" type or the "combination". Most issues to do with relationships are hard to define and don't have a unique, let alone foolproof, solution. Some of our difficulties may also be "icebergs" in that the roots of the issue are to be found in attitudes that go back many years; we are therefore very unlikely to get to the bottom line quickly.

Another important message for us has emerged from research about both creativity and the management of change. There is a clear link between the number of options that we consider and the resulting capacity to change. Presenting only one option may well produce an argument. Even two alternatives often lead to black-and-white thinking without an increased commitment to either outcome. Do you remember the rhetoric that accompanied the UK government's introduction of the poll tax, apart from the reaction to selecting Scotland for the pilot scheme? We were told that the system was "better than the rates". While that might have been true, many people were left with a feeling of dissatisfaction. We had a sense that if somebody had thought for long enough, there were other alternatives preferable to either of the options presented to us so far. In terms of our commitment to change, two alternatives are not much better than one.

On the other hand, we could brainstorm interminably and produce too many ideas. That scenario usually produces an overwhelming sense of "Goodness, where on earth do we start?" Too many options are as counter-productive as too few. Somewhere between these two extremes lies the best result; consider a range of options and make a selection. Sometimes we can implement more than one approach simultaneously. I've summarized this link on the graph below; notice that there are no numbers on either axis. How many options should we ideally generate? It depends on personality and the type of problem. My principal reason for including this section is to encourage you to recognize and consider a number of possible approaches, especially to problems that are centred on human relationships.

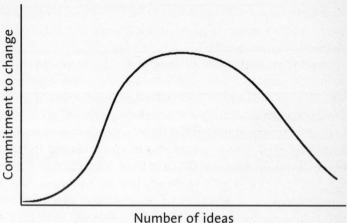

We need to be careful to distinguish between the awkward behaviour of an individual, or even a few people, as opposed to a difficult group norm. Admittedly, group patterns of behaviour are only comprised of the activity of individual members, but there may be better or worse alternative solutions, depending on the depth of the problem. For example, you may have one or two group members who talk too much and too often, to the exclusion of the rest of the group. Or perhaps the problem is more widespread, where virtually all of the group have strong opinions and would like to air them rather than listen to other people. The two scenarios require quite different approaches, even if the group problem has been primarily caused by allowing a few individuals a little too much rope. If the difficulty is limited, then a few quiet words may suffice; with a wider problem we might have to introduce techniques like going round the room to hear "answers" in rotation. When the behaviour of an individual is disruptive, ask yourself whether the issue might be best sorted within the meeting context or on a private basis external to the gathering.

Rebel or leader?

There is one personality that we should consider at this stage, the apparent rebel. I want to encourage you to persevere with such people. At first sight, the rebel is the last person that we want in any group, but at least they are not ultra-passive! Deep inside them however, there may be a strong desire to influence, which is unfulfilled and frustrated at present. Potentially these rebels are the interns and small-group leaders of the future. Usually there are character and security issues to be sorted out before we would give them any formal position, but they usually have strong leadership drives. They represent a different challenge to us from the sober, upright person, who is never any trouble, but will never lead a horse to water either! We need these rebels, provided that their behaviour is not dramatically disruptive. Pray them in, pray for them and pray over them (with their permission!). Too often, the temptation is to attempt to meet fire with fire; now that really will lead to a serious conflict, probably a battle of wills and possibly even a lost member. Don't take every challenge personally; don't expect and never demand total compliance.

My experience tells me very clearly that many general difficulties that are apparently outside our control might have been avoided, or the damage minimized, if the preparation had been better. Many of our potential problems within small groups can also be avoided with a little preparation, some thinking in advance. Typical sources of such problems include:

Wrong expectations
Late changes in the practical arrangements like day of the
    week, time or venue
Too small/big a group
Too much/little content for the evening
A greater than usual spread of maturity within the group.

Potentially these sorts of difficulties are best solved by a bit
of disciplined preparation (often including better communication). A danger can be that we assume that most problems are about relationship issues. Often the roots are
structures, systems and administration. Make sure that we
use both verbal announcements and written reinforcement
of administrative detail. Not only is the prayer cover obviously critical, but it might be worth asking yourself some
questions like:

What might be the controversial elements this evening?
Whose behaviour might be difficult?
What are my absolute minimum expectations of this
    evening?
What parts of the discussion have more than one valid per-
    spective?
On which elements of the evening should we spend the most
    time?

Questions like this are worth considering in advance. They
encourage our prayer life and the answers may prevent
inflammatory reactions on our behalf to the "unpredictable" type of problem.

Sometimes apparent difficulties will be linked to real
gifts in the members, in a similar manner to the
rebel/leader. For example, the person who wants to turn all
summer meetings into social events is likely to have strong
needs for informal relationships. You can see their behaviour as potentially disruptive or focus on the possibility
that they might bring a vital ingredient of acceptance and

listening to the group dynamics. Their strength and weakness come out of the same stem. With strengths will also come allowable weaknesses, which we have to live with and accept. However, there will be levels of difficulty parallel to each strength which given free rein, would be damaging to the life of the group as a whole. Let's illustrate the problem further. Somebody with a potential teaching ministry might make each of their contributions too long and go into unproductive detail and the "real meaning" of the Greek or Hebrew! We need to help them to contribute more succinctly, without crushing the gift or failing to benefit from their knowledge.

In management training at work, some of you might have seen videos starring John Cleese. The key points are often memorably made by doing the wrong things to such an exaggerated extent that the consequences are ridiculous. Instead of doing things partially correctly, he makes a total mess of things so that we can more clearly see the impact of mediocre standards. Let's try and use the same approach for running a small-group meeting:

Recipe for a disastrous small-group evening

1. Let the programme limp from week to week with no shared vision.
2. Assume that the group can fulfil all possible purposes, every week.
3. Give the minimum notice to a few people and trust that they will spread the word.
4. Go either at the pace of the least or most mature.
5. Answer every phone call during the meeting.
6. Pay no attention to room layout, temperature and refreshments.
7. Know your full agenda and steer the discussion to your own conclusions.
8. Encourage as many people as possible to attend your group; it proves what a good group leader you are.

9. Assume that non-attendance is definitely down to lack of commitment.
10. Start late and finish very late indeed.
11. Trust that the Spirit will guide to such an extent that preparation is a waste of time.
12. Use as much jargon as possible and make sure that new people are aware of their ignorance when they can't find the right passage.
13. It is of vital importance that nobody enjoys themselves.
14. Make sure that the programme has no links to other activities within the church.
15. All disagreements should be refereed by you and either swept under the carpet or fought to a standstill.
16. Report back to the minister/elder that you had a great time, again!

Remember that we are in a spiritual battle. The growth and sanctification in our lives brings no pleasure to the "opposition". You can't expect leading a small group to be all plain sailing. When you first look at problems within the group, presume that you can do something about them, and that most tricky situations are unproductive. We are all experiencing enough conflict in our lives already. Look for beneficial outcomes and look for sustainable solutions.

Chapter **14**   *Evaluating the Small Group*

You may have noticed that a consistent theme in this book is my desire to see improvement in the lives of every individual, including the leaders. The same desire should be true of every small group. Almost whatever the present standard of any aspect of church that we choose to consider, it is probably more important to know whether things are getting better or worse. The gradient, if you like, is of more interest than the height. I have written extensively about the biblical basis of evaluation and the skills of personal appraisals in my previous book and will not repeat those details. Suffice to say that the principles of evaluation are frequently illustrated from Genesis 1 (the creation account) to Revelation 2 and 3 (the letters to the seven churches). Evaluation, looking for improvement, is a positive activity and is not judgemental.

Evaluating the effectiveness of a group or a team is technically much more difficult than evaluating the performance of an individual, and for a variety of reasons. First, there are extra dimensions to be looked at, like cohesion, relationships and dynamics. These issues do not come into play within the process of personal evaluation. Secondly, shared group goals are more difficult to identify and agree than individual targets. Finally, and most importantly, there will be different perspectives on any outcomes; every individual within a group will have their own opinion. In particular, the leader has an important opinion, but there is a danger that undue weight is attached to their view. Later when we look at a practical tool we will need to take care that the views of members as well as leaders can be taken into account. You may not be surprised to hear that the leaders of small groups often have a more positive perspective on the situation than their members!

I am frequently asked to visit churches, organizations or teams to conduct an audit, an evaluation or a review. (These three words are often used interchangeably.) The invitation usually means "Come and give us the once over"! Immediately, there must be some dialogue. My first question is usually, "Tell me where you are itching." Nobody asks for an external review unless there is an area of dissatisfaction. The same should be true in a small-group scenario. The tools may be less sophisticated, less expensive and quicker to apply, but the reasons for an audit need to be the same. Which areas cause us most concern? How can we improve further?

The second key question is "Against what do you want to be measured?" and asking that question has cost me a few jobs! Subjective assessments without previously agreed yardsticks are likely to yield less information. What are the criteria for assessing good churches, teams and groups? Should I be comparing you with the best church that I have visited, the worst, or my own? The answer must involve something about the vision. Too many evaluations look at yesterday's problems and the solutions are therefore bound to be late when they are eventually put into place. We have, to some extent, to second-guess the future so that our corrective actions meet tomorrow's needs not just yesterday's. At the very minimum, the purpose of the group must be clearly identified; assessing a Bible-study group is bound to be very different from analysing a group in a cell church. Any reasonable attempt at an evaluation requires that the criteria for measurement were put in place in advance, so that we can now ask, "How are we doing?"

It's also worth thinking about the frequency of the audit of your group. There needs to be a link between the calibre of the tool, and therefore the time taken to use it, and the frequency of application. Nobody is suggesting taking a whole meeting per month to analyse progress but a substantial check-up needs to be done every so often. Like most other life principles, you will get out according to what you put in, up to a certain level of investment. A quick glance may reveal some early warning signs; a better tool will give you a more detailed response. At the end of this chapter, there is a tool for you to use in your group. It is designed to have a general application, but will have shortfalls because it is not tailor made for your context. Adapt it as you see fit!

The frequency of auditing needs also to depend on the purpose of the group. In the strictest cell climate, groups are often disbanded after a year if they have not multiplied. In a Bible-study group, continuity is prized more highly, so the rate of change will be slower. In cells, I recommend reviews approximately with the school terms, about every four months. In a Bible-study group, "results" are probably deemed less important than softer analysis; once a year might well suffice.

Good evaluation requires a statement of purpose, values and vision. We also need a concept to bridge the gap in scale between the vision and the week-to-week activities. Thrusts are a crucial tool and help us to focus on the medium time frame. They answer the question "What are the four or five major areas of activity that will move us from where we are, to where we want to be?" Phrased another way: "What four or five initiatives should we be addressing in the next review period that will move us an appropriate distance towards the vision?"

Each broad thrust should have subordinate goals. Goal statements must meet the following conditions:

S pecific
M easurable
A ttractive
R ealistic
T imed

It might be useful for you to imagine thrusts and goals as the next items moving down the flow chart near the end of Chapter 9. Setting out these components at the start of the time span is the key to the quality of the review. We need to determine in advance what the success criteria will be. If we cannot measure outcomes, we will not know which areas warrant improvement. Your understanding of the answers to these elements of forward thinking should be your sub-conscious database as you work through the questionnaire.

All self-score numerical questionnaires are subjective by their very nature. The purpose of this tool is to elicit your views, but more importantly, to generate group discussion. Although any group leader could work through the questionnaire alone, I would strongly prefer that the group members all complete the tool individually and then discuss their answers together.

An audit tool

Score each statement according to this five point scale:

5 points	I strongly agree
4 points	I agree
3 points	I am not sure, I am near the borderline between agree and disagree
2 points	I disagree
1 point	I strongly disagree *or* I don't know

Please put the scores in the spaces by each statement. The score should reflect your personal perspective, not what you think the other members of the group would score.

A Content   Score

The content of most evenings is worthwhile. _____

The content is applicable to our everyday lives. _____

The balance of the ingredients reflects our purpose
    and vision. _____

I do not feel that there are major deficiencies in the
    overall church programme. _____

We continue with themes of content long enough
    that I can see tangible results. _____

B Process

The pace of the evenings holds my attention. _____

Members do have a say in how the evenings are
    conducted. _____

We start and finish on time. _____

There is a good link and flow across the ingredients
    of the evening. _____

We use a range of teaching methods that actually
    produce learning. _____

C Relationships

It is possible to disagree without losing relationship. _____

Relationships within the group are excellent. _____

Difficulties are resolved quickly. _____

Negative humour is not focused on particular
    individuals. _____

The depth of sharing illustrates real trust between
    the members. _____

D Contributions

All members make a contribution every week. _____

All contributions are respected on merit, whoever
    makes them. _____

Contributions are relevant to the discussion. _____

If we lose the direction in a discussion, we come
    back on track quickly. _____

We are good at summarizing and reaching
conclusions. _____

E Values
The church has a clear statement of its core values. _____
New members will quickly find behavioural evidence
of these stated values. _____
Our small group operates in a manner that is
consistent with the values of the wider church. _____
Behaviour which contradicts the core values is soon
challenged. _____
I am comfortable with the strong emphasis that we
place on these core values. _____

F Vision
We all know why this group exists and what we are
here to do. _____
We all know the vision of this church. _____
Our small group has a clear sense of direction. _____
The group's vision is utterly consistent with the
wider church. _____
We have clear short-term goals which stem from
the vision. _____

G Effectiveness
We have a sense of progress from one month to the
next. _____
We regularly evaluate our progress. _____
We "celebrate" the things that have gone well. _____
We have grown numerically since our last review. _____
The group has multiplied in the last twelve months. _____

H Community
The group members support each other in various
ways outside the formal meeting. _____

Folk from the group spend time together frequently outside the formal meeting. ____

There are natural friendships as well as functional relationships. ____

We care for one another, rather than expecting the group leader to solely do the caring. ____

We are not a clique; new people are readily accepted and we make space for them. ____

I Leadership

I feel secure in this leader's group. ____

The use of authority is wise and appropriate. ____

Discussions flow naturally and not all the contributions have to be directed through the leader. ____

The leader's heart is much more for the group than their own personal fulfilment. ____

Sufficient authority is delegated when we are asked to do things. ____

J Personal development

I know that I have matured considerably as a direct result of my involvement in this group. ____

There are clear expectations of changes that we should implement in our lives after each meeting. ____

There are clear expectations that members will disciple others and be discipled. ____

There are always interns in the group, people who are being prepared for future leadership. ____

People are given opportunity to do challenging things, not just mundane chores. ____

Add up your scores for each section and record them on this score sheet. There is a maximum of 25 points per section. Chart up the scores so that the whole group can see all of the scores to every section. Look for three main features which will generate discussion about any given section:

1. If most people have given low scores to a section, then that area obviously needs attention. There is no absolute range for "What is a low score?" It is a relative term, among your other scores.

2. If the scores for a section are generally high, but one or two people have given that section a particularly low score, explore their reasons. Don't write off the scores that fail to fit the pattern as statistical anomalies!

3. Celebrate the areas where you are agreed about the high scores!

Score sheet

Section	Total points
A. Content	____
B. Process	____
C. Relationships	____
D. Contributions	____
E. Values	____
F. Vision	____
G. Effectiveness	____
H. Community	____
I. Leadership	____
J. Personal development	____

At the end of any sort of review there are two principal dangers: trying to improve everything at once, and alternatively, after much thought of course, doing nothing! As a result of your discussions, select two sections for improvement. Commit yourselves to four goals (SMART format) which will have a major impact on the sections that you have chosen.

Conclusion

In summary, I want to draw together some key points from this book. We have talked about improving our communication skills; there is every possibility, and written communication is particularly vulnerable to misinterpretation, that what you read and understood is not what I thought I wrote! The following principles underpin the practical advice that we have explored, a sort of "ten commandments".

1. Small groups are an integral part of most "successful" churches

The vast majority of churches that would be deemed "lively" and "successful" place a considerable emphasis on small groups, which can be structured in a variety of different ways. These groups are helping to meet a need expressed by many people — the desire for meaningful relationships and a sense of community.

2. Work at the skills of small-group leadership

Many leadership development approaches have placed such an emphasis on character and knowledge that skill training has been virtually ignored. Leaders often have an inflated opinion of their skills, especially in regarding their communication skills as peerless! It's always possible to improve in these skills and even a small increment will pay substantial dividends.

3. Train plenty of leaders

Many churches experience a shortage of small-group leaders. We underestimate the "natural wastage" of people moving away, tiredness, and other demands on their time.

There needs to be a permanent commitment to the training and releasing of new leaders. Depending on the structure, small-group leadership need not be too exacting, and is an ideal opportunity for an initial experience of leadership.

4. Cell-church thinking has made a significant impact on small-group activity

The cell-church phenomenon has given a real impetus to many churches and their small groups. The benefits have often been via an increased emphasis on discipleship and numerical growth. What is meant by "cell" and the level of adoption of pure cell principles varies enormously. I have increasingly heard "We are a church with cells, not a cell church." Sometimes in "churches with cells", there is little discernible difference compared with what was being done before, namely a version of homegroups. Not surprisingly, the benefits are correspondingly small.

5. Emphasize life not structure

There is a danger of focusing too much on the structures of small groups, rather than the life that should be produced by such groups. Ultimately, people have the right to vote, with their feet, and they decide for themselves whether a group is worth attending. Fun and enjoyment will prove at least as important as duty and commitment, if we are truly looking for a response of the heart and not just attendance and compliance.

6. It is a major culture change for small groups to be part of the church's evangelism

Groups can only be deemed outward looking if the individual members are outward looking. Our inability to share the gospel within natural one-to-one relationships limits our evangelism, and I believe the reasons are primarily cultural. Very few small groups are consistently geared towards new members, in either their thinking or their programmes.

7. We must be clear about the purpose and values of our groups

It is critical that small groups know the purpose for their existence and that they hold and exhibit the same values as the wider church. I have frequently found that clarity on these issues has transformed the quality of group life.

8. Every group needs a vision

Too often, the programme limps from week to week without a clear sense of shared vision and direction. For activity to become meaningful, the programme of each week needs to be visibly integrated into a bigger picture. Groups need their own vision, under the corporate umbrella of the bigger church.

9. There are a variety of causes, approaches and solutions to relationship problems

Leaders need to be flexible in how they respond to difficulties with members and among members. Issues are often about values and seldom about personality. Remember that we can observe behaviour, but it is dangerous to attribute motives before exploration.

10. The key model of pastoral care in the New Testament is "one anothering"

Small groups are a positive forum for expressing good support and encouragement, as well as teaching, learning and worshipping. We need to change the mentality that the leader pastors the flock.

Bibliography

Jeffrey Arnold, *The Big Book on Small Groups* (IVP: Leicester, 1992), 0-8308-1377-2.

Howard Astin, *Body and Cell* (Monarch Books: Mill Hill, 1998), 1-85424-409-4.

Ian Coffey and Stephen Gaukroger, eds, *Housegroups: the leaders' survival guide* (Crossway Books, 1996), 1-85684-148-0.

David Cormack, *Change Directions* (Monarch Books: Mill Hill, 1995), 1-85424-310-1.

Peter Cotterell, *All About House Groups* (Kingsway, Eastbourne, 1985), 0-86065-361-7.

Em Griffin, *Getting Together* (IVP, Leicester, 1982), 0-87784-390-2.

Bryn Hughes, *Leadership Tool Kit* (Monarch Books: Crowborough, 1998), 1-85424-377-2.

Jimmy Long, *Generating Hope: reaching the postmodern generation* (Marshall Pickering, 1997), 0-55103199-9.

C J Mahaney, ed., *Why Small Groups?* (People of destiny, 1996), 1-881039-06-4.

John Mallison, *Growing Christians in Small Groups* (Scripture Union: London, 1989), 0-86201-583-9.

Neal F McBride, *How to Lead Small Groups* (NavPress, 1990), 0-89109-303-6.

Neal F McBride, *Small groups don't just happen* (NavPress, 1998), 1-57683-103-5.

Ralph Neighbour, *Where do we go from here?* (Touch Publications, 1990), 1-880828-54-5.

Laurence Singlehurst and Liz West, *Moving to Cells* (Cell Church UK, 2000), 1-902144-05-8.

Larry Stockstill, *The Cell Church* (Regal, Gospel Light, USA, 1998), 0-8307-2133-9.

Ron Trudinger, *Cells for Life* (The Olive Tree Publications, 1979), 906645-01-8.

David Yonggi Cho, *Successful Home Cell Groups* (Bridge-Logos Publishers, NY, USA, 1981), 0-88270-513-X.